UNLOCKING YOUR

INNER
ZELENSKY

Also by Jessie Asya Kanzer

Don't Just Sit There, DO NOTHING

UNLOCKING YOUR
INNER
ZELENSKY

LESSONS WE CAN ALL LEARN
FROM AN UNEXPECTED LEADER

Jessie Asya Kanzer

ST. MARTIN'S
ESSENTIALS
NEW YORK

First published in the United States by St. Martin's Essentials,
an imprint of St. Martin's Publishing Group

www.stmartins.com

Designed by Steven Seighman

The Library of Congress Cataloging-in-Publication Data is available
upon request.

ISBN 978-1-250-89476-2 (trade paperback)
ISBN 978-1-250-89477-9 (ebook)

Our books may be purchased in bulk for promotional, educational,
or business use. Please contact your local bookseller or the Macmillan
Corporate and Premium Sales Department at 1-800-221-7945, extension
5442, or by email at MacmillanSpecialMarkets@macmillan.com.

First Edition: 2023

10 9 8 7 6 5 4 3 2 1

*In honor of all those who lost their lives in Ukraine
in the fight for freedom and humanity.
May their memory be a blessing.*

Contents

Note

You may notice that the title of this book, *Unlocking Your Inner Zelensky*, has one *y* in the Ukrainian president's name. Yet within the chapters, you'll find the spelling of Zelenskyy with the double *y* at the end. And you may wonder *Why*?

The thing is, while it's often a challenge to spell a non-English name in English in a way that best captures its pronunciation, it's doubly challenging when two non-English languages and an imperialistic past (and present attempt) are involved. The president is widely referred to as *Zelensky*, including in the *New York Times*. But I've also heard the argument that the single *y* spelling reflects a more Russian approach, with the double *y* being an approximation that's closer to Ukrainian. And the president's own Twitter handle is @ZelenskyyUa. So . . . we've made room for both.

He's largely known as *Zelensky* but seems to prefer *Zelenskyy*, and we're paying deference to that. Because, sometimes, a dig at tyranny can be found in as small a detail as a double *y*.

Preface

"Do you think Zelenskyy is ready to lead his country through war?" I was asked repeatedly in the weeks leading up to Russia's brutal attack on Ukraine—mostly because I appeared in his movie once and I too hail from the former Soviet Union.

"Is anyone ready for war?" I'd answer with a smirk. My own grandfather was a World War II hero from Ukraine; both my grandmothers survived the Holocaust.

Folks were understandably concerned about Volodymyr Zelenskyy's lack of serious political experience—he was an actor and comedian before becoming president (and a great dancer, I should add: Have you seen his *Dancing with the Stars* win?). War is serious, though; comedy is . . . well, comedy. Yet from the moment Russia invaded his country in the early morning of Thursday, February 24, 2022, Zelenskyy showed us that laughter and tears come from the same source: humanity. And he is a master human.

As I listened to Zelenskyy speak in Ukrainian, as well as in my—and his—native Russian tongue, with such authentic emotion, such passion for all the freedoms we sometimes take for granted, I finally understood why I'd been so drawn to his story. I understood why I was compelled to dedicate to his masterhood an entire chapter in my first book, which, ironically, was released in those shocking first days of the war. "*My* Zelenskyy" I'd referred to him then, not realizing he would become *our* Zelenskyy.

But everything began to make sense to me as I watched this man in awe, together with the rest of the world: Why I, a spiritual searcher whose Jewish Ukrainian grandfather fought alongside Zelenskyy's Jewish Ukrainian grandfather, crossed paths with the man. I understood why I couldn't stop writing about him. Far more important, I understood why this comedic actor was propelled into the role of president just in time to lead his people through unimaginable terror.

You see, Volodymyr Zelenskyy isn't simply a great wartime politician or Ukraine's remarkable leader. He isn't even the "leader of the free world," which is what American news channels started calling him—or, rather, he's not *just* that. I believe Zelenskyy is a profound philosophical leader of our generation—one who'd been underestimated many a time—and that his influence goes far beyond "the West" or "the free world" or any other titles humans use to mark "us" and "them." In fact, Zelenskyy was as quickly venerated in Afghanistan as he was in Europe, Afghanis saying they wished they'd had such a leader to guide them through their suffering.

Without trying to be, perhaps without even fully understanding his role, Zelenskyy, much like *The Matrix*'s Neo,
was fated to show us the Way. . . . Which brings me back
to my own way, the one I was hobbling to find for years
after immigrating to America from Soviet Latvia, where I
was born. And twenty years into my American journey, I
happened to cross paths with the Ukrainian Neo.

In 2009, Zelenskyy, then simply a comedian, was headlining his first big film, part of which was shooting in New
York. This Russian rom-com called *Love in the Big City* was
about Russian expats dating up a storm in the Big Apple. It
featured leads from various countries that'd once been part
of the Soviet bloc. Bit parts in the film, meanwhile, went to
actual expats like me—Soviet-born immigrants hustling for
a version of the American dream. Whether you were there
or here, the need to hustle remained. Still, it was fun to play
in my childhood language as a grown-up.

After shooting this movie—having portrayed the for-
gettable role of "girl in sports club #1," the lines I was to
speak in Russian cut—I went on with my frustrating hustle until, eventually, I threw in the towel. I got a regular job, married a lovely American man, and settled down
in a lovely American town. Zelenskyy, on the other hand,
skyrocketed to stardom in a Ukrainian sitcom called *Servant of the People*, where he played a teacher who spoke
out against dishonesty and became president. But then—
here's the craziest part—he decided to run for president in
real life, calling his party Servant of the People, no less.
And . . . he won.

Ze, as he's been nicknamed, charmed his country with

his wit, his charisma, his irreverent talent. Seriously, look up "Zelenskyy playing piano with his balls." It's not as dirty as it sounds, I promise.

But also, the guy brilliantly used comedy as a tool to tell the truth—to point at what needed to change in Ukrainian politics and society, and to imagine an alternative. He was elected to the very position he'd portrayed on TV, yes. But also—whether skillfully or fortuitously—he positioned himself in a role where he could effect the change he'd been intimating for years.

We all know what happened after that, though: war. Well, not immediately. First Zelenskyy was weirdly caught in the middle of an American scandal—remember? It was his conversation with President Trump that was at the center of Trump's impeachment trial. Did the then US president attempt to blackmail Ze into digging up dirt on Joe Biden's son, who'd done business in Ukraine? Did he withhold aid and a meeting very much desired by Zelenskyy?

Trump was to the left of Ze, Putin to the right, and Zelenskyy did his best to keep his head up and to bring the focus back to the needs of his nation—which had already been at war with Russia in Donbas since 2014, with Putin having already illegally annexed Crimea. But these details wouldn't come to the world's attention until later.

Fact is, most of us knew—and cared—little about Ukraine before the maniacal Putin full-on invaded it in February 2022. Then, suddenly, we realized the awesomeness of this former Soviet republic that was a buffer between Russia and the rest of Europe—this nation that badly wanted to integrate into Europe, but one that Putin believed belonged to Russia. Suddenly we realized the intense difficulty of leading Ukraine . . . and the intense man who had traded a very successful entertainment career to lead it.

So if I could go back in time a bit to answer the question, "Do you think Zelenskyy is ready to lead his country through war?" I would say, "Um . . . Yes, have you seen him? Ukrainian Neo is ready to lead us all."

I must add a bold caveat here—so more like CAVEAT. I don't have a crystal ball to show me where Zelenskyy, Ukraine, Europe, and Russia will net out in five, ten, twenty years. Obviously, my hope is with the people of Ukraine and with Volodymyr Zelenskyy. I believe in them and in him. Just like you, I am in awe of this leader, this nation—of his profundity and humanity, of their collective bravery.

The dangers and forces Ukraine is up against are mind-numbing. But its only option for survival is victory. How will these two realities co-create Ukraine's future (fingers crossed)? I do not know.

However, this book's lessons from Zelenskyy are not dependent on a perfect ending. They form a guide all their own, for whichever season you're living through—the toughest and the not-so-tough—and whatever obstacles you are up against.

Zelenskyy's moral clarity is so remarkable that it can serve us regardless of what's happening in our own story lines—and no matter what happens in his. And because I've watched him long enough, I have no doubt that it will continue to lead him.

It is this clarity, by the way, that I'm referring to when I refer to your *Inner Zelenskyy* and to unlocking it.

Because this Inner Zelenskyy can change your life.

UNLOCKING YOUR
INNER
ZELENSKY

Who the *Bleep*...?

I don't care what nationality a person is—what's important is who he is on the inside.

—*Zelenskyy speaking to a group of Russian journalists*
on March 27, 2022 (most of them operating outside
Russia at that point)

Who am I? is a question we all think about occasionally. And for many of us, it's a puzzle we struggle to piece together our entire lives. Is our identity the country we come from? The religion we follow? The language we speak? Essentially, we are asking what makes us . . . us.

How to define myself—the Soviet "Asya Bronfman," the

Americanized "Jessie Kanzer," and everything in between—has always plagued me. But never more than during the war Russia launched in Ukraine, with many people from my part of the world suddenly asking themselves the same thing.

"I am Russian," I used to say, because that's how I thought of myself, I guess—or, rather, how I thought it would be easy for others to think of me—until Vladimir Putin turned *Russian* into an icky word. *Russian* began to mean aggressor, savage, bully, as if overnight. Except, of course, there were plenty of Russian people who didn't align with that definition in the least—an identity that had been hijacked by Putin and Co., gradually and then all of a sudden.

Ukrainian president Volodymyr Zelenskyy, however, was here to help us view identity differently.

Perhaps for every Vladimir we are given a Volodymyr.

Volodymyr

When Zelenskyy first ran for president of Ukraine in 2019, he was heavily criticized by his opponents for being a comic without political experience. This was predictable—he had been known as a comedian, actor, producer, and even as an entertainment magnate, until then. It was a strange about-face, to say the least. Ze was certainly astute in the comedic work he created, and he easily highlighted the absurdity of his nation's political quagmire . . . but was that translatable to a presidency?

Once he was elected—in a landslide—he was especially

mocked by Russian media for not fitting the quasi-macho politician mold that was their norm. "He is weak," said Russian commentator Sergey Parkhomenko. "He has no religion, he has no nationality."

Alas, this commentator had misread Zelenskyy's lack of ego-domination for weakness, his lack of religiosity for a lack of faith, and his linguistic flexibility (he grew up speaking Russian, and then learned both Ukrainian and English) for a lack of nationality. Not to mention that in leading his nation, Zelenskyy's focus was *not* on his own identity.

Ze believed that power should always lie in the hands of civilized people, rather than in the hands of tyrants—that a politician should carry out the will of these people, rather than the other way around. And he believed that who he was should never overshadow his job of representing his citizens. Perhaps most significantly he showed us all that being Ukrainian did not depend on what language you spoke, on your ethnicity, or on your religion—or lack thereof, and that we can all aim to be a little bit Ukrainian—at least when it comes to mental fortitude.

In several of his wartime interviews, Zelenskyy reminded folks that Ukraine is home to one hundred different ethnicities, pointing out that now, they were all united as a single force for good.

Blue and Yellow

"Who else had the courage to persuade the largest global companies to forget about accounting and recall morality?"

Zelenskyy asked his people in an April 2022 address, "And to teach all political leaders—whatever they are—to be at least a little Ukrainian . . . At least a little brave." And suddenly many of us around the world began displaying blue and yellow flags, whatever and whomever we were.

Ze expanded *Ukrainian* to mean more than just the ethnicity that's native to the land; his entire country gave new meaning to the word. In fact, there were plenty of ethnically Russian inhabitants of Ukraine who followed their president's lead and stood up for freedom—like Ivan Fedorov, the mayor of the city of Melitopol, who was kidnapped by Russian troops when he refused to cooperate with their takeover. (He was later released in a prisoner exchange.)

As we saw in the war—as Zelenskyy himself explained—to be Ukrainian meant to be a free people who came together and stood up for one another, a people who oversaw their own country and didn't bend down to autocracy. If you lived in Ukraine, if you believed in freedom and democracy, you were Ukrainian—whether your family originated in Russia, or were Jewish like Zelenskyy's, or whether you had Korean roots like Vitaliy Kim, the governor of Ukraine's Mykolaiv, in whose capital city some of my own relatives still reside.

Being Ukrainian became an ideal, a set of beliefs.

What a forward way of thinking, I realized—to get to choose your own identity based on the way you want to live your life, rather than having it be predetermined by your ethnicity, your religion, or the language you speak; there were thousands upon thousands of Ukrainians whose mother tongue was Russian.

Zelenskyy showed us that our identities are more than just the geopolitical stuff which happened before our birth or which lies outside our control. He showed us that we can choose better than what surrounds us.

"Even in the darkest of circumstances, there are people who carry light," Zelenskyy said on May 14, 2022, the Day of Remembrance of Ukrainians who saved Jews in World War II. And he demonstrated that it's this light that matters most—the very light he helped ignite and keep lit in Ukraine during its greatest struggle.

"We are defending the ability of a person to live in the modern world," Ze said in an interview with *60 Minutes* in April 2022. "We are defending the right to live."

"These are human values," he explained, "so that Russia doesn't choose what we should do and how I'm exercising my rights. That right was given to me by God and my parents."

Questions

Identity is a theme—a right—that is complex for displaced and oppressed people alike, born into a society we would change if we had the choice. But even after leaving an oppressive country, realizing that we at least get to choose who we are as individuals often takes years.

"You left because Russia was not freedom?" my kindergartener asked me around the time the war in Ukraine began. She was trying to put together the bits and pieces I had delved out to her in her young life—the young life I had no desire to sully with reality quite yet.

"Yes, except I didn't leave Russia," I said. "I left Latvia, which was ruled by Russia."

"But Baba and DeeDee are Russian?" she continued.

"No, DeeDee [her version of *deda*, which is Russian for "grandpa"] is from Ukraine and Baba is from Siberia—which *is* Russia, but her family was sent there from Latvia.

"Plus, we're Jewish," I added for posterity, not that there was any five-year-old attention span left for me and my origins at that point.

The thing is, I used to tell my kids I *was* Russian. After all, I spoke Russian and I sang Russian lullabies, not to mention, I'd been called Russian ever since I came to America.

I had no idea how to explain the truth of it all without explaining the truth of it *all*. But when Russia invaded Ukraine, I tried.

"Well, why doesn't someone just kill the guy?" my almost-eight-year-old asked incredulously, referring to Putin.

"Is Russia still trying to be the boss of where you're from?" the kindergartner piped in.

And again, I was out of answers.

Personal History

While I was born in Riga, Latvia, under Soviet rule, it simply said "Jew" on my family's passports (not that I had any idea what *Jew* meant until after I left the USSR).

And I know that on my first trip out of Riga, we visited my dad's family in different parts of Ukraine—various aunts overfeeding me in jovial Odessa and in my father's hometown of Vinnytsya. I remember going by train a couple of years later with my mom and her friend to Saint Petersburg, still called Leningrad then. We saw my mom's uncle, who had settled there, and we took in the museums, the architecture, the old European beauty.

Of course, I have countless memories of Riga, with its old-city cobblestone streets and the apartment complexes on its outskirts that I saw mirrored in the blown-up ones in Ukraine. We'd resided on the ninth floor. And now I could feel the ruined dream of every ruined flat. My family had lived that dream—an apartment all our own—after years in my babushka's Soviet communal one, with its rusty bathtub in the kitchen, a single toilet and rotary phone, all shared by random occupants.

We got the chance to emigrate during perestroika. After several refugee months in Europe, we landed in Brooklyn. Coming here on the heels of the Cold War, I was marked "Russian" by my American classmates, who didn't understand the complex truth of my part of the world. It was 1989 and Russophobia was all the rage.

"Where are you rushin', Russian?" they'd ask mockingly in the stairwell.

Russian became the easier thing to call myself. I was my friends' "Russian friend," then my husband's "Russian wife," and so on. I didn't much mind. I'd think wistfully of the Russian cartoons of my youth—the songs, the stories— the very same ones that my peers consumed, whether they were in Odessa, in Leningrad, or in my birthplace of Riga. There was no choice for anything else, really, in the days of

Soviet domination. There was a comfort in that, much like a caged animal finds comfort in small spaces.

Still, as I grew up in New York, I mostly shed the Russianness instilled in me in my state-run day-care days. I changed my name from *Asya* to *Jessie*. I stopped reading Russian books; I relaxed my Soviet rigidity day by day. Freedom creeps in with a one-way ticket.

I became so free, in fact, I didn't choose a practical career—the kind that was touted by most immigrant parents (business, law, accounting). But amusingly, as an actress/waitress in my twenties, I found myself hanging out with quintessential Russian producers on the set of their movie *Love in the Big City*—the movie that starred an up-and-coming Ukrainian comedian named Volodymyr Zelenskyy. He was on his way to glory; I was on my way to quitting. He took center stage as a playboy dentist, while I, "girl in sports club #1," lingered off set, drinking the copious champagne the Russian producers poured me.

"You could make it if you just do something with your nose and your chin," one of them told me. She wasn't a fan of my Semitic nose, I guess; I still don't know what she had against my chin.

As I moved on with my life, first relocating to LA, then back to New York, I fell even more out of touch with the Russian language and culture and food. Though later, when I nursed my sweet American babes, Russian bedtime songs would escape my lips, tone-deaf as I was. It was the Russian character of Cheburashka that I told them about—a toy that didn't know who he was or where he belonged.

During the initial days of terror in Ukraine, as I was glued to my iPhone, listening to Volodymyr Zelenskyy's nightly addresses, making sure first thing in the morning, like all of us gaga Ze fans, that he was still alive . . . well . . . it's not that I got a better idea of who I was, necessarily, but rather that I became more cognizant of who I was *not*. I became ever more aware of the cruel tyranny I came from, which my family miraculously survived. My grandfather who fought the Nazis; my grandmother who ran for her life, bombs falling at her heels. My other set of grandparents who came up in the shadows of the Stalin gulags, where their parents had been locked up as punishment for nonexistent crimes—along with millions upon millions of Soviet citizens-victims.

It may be where I was born—in the Soviet Union—but I am not Soviet. Nor am I Russian (though Cheburashka will always have a place in my heart). So now I make sure to correct my kids when they refer to me as Russian, and I correct my American friends. Sometimes I correct myself. I may speak Russian, but my identity is more complicated.

And anyway, as Volodymyr Zelenskyy reminded us, it's who a person is "on the inside" that matters.

I guess I would say, on the inside, I'm a citizen of the world. Yet there is a big part of me that's American, and another part that is Ukrainian (a proud half, to be precise) . . . one that is Latvian (another half), and also "Jew," as my family passports had read. I'm an American Jewish Ukrainian Latvian citizen of the world. And I left because Russia was not freedom.

And anyway, as Volodymyr Zelenskyy reminded me, no matter where I was born or what happens in the country I call home, *I* say who I am and I get to define it. As do you.

Choice

In one wartime recording, Zelenskyy spoke to an elderly woman from Mariupol whose granddaughter had been orphaned and injured in the war. She was so grateful for his attention and for the assistance she received from the Ukrainian army in finding and getting help for the girl. "I'm just in shock," she said in Russian. "Me, a regular woman, getting so much assistance. . . . Thank you!"

Volodymyr Zelenskyy looked her straight in the eye and said, "But we are all regular people," though the right translation for the Russian word he used is closer to "simple."

"We are all simple people," he said. And we really are, aren't we? No matter what our labels or titles, we're all simply human.

"I don't care what nationality a person is," Zelenskyy had told Russian journalists, "what's important is who he is on the inside."

Isn't that what we should all focus on?

And while, say, a Russian person is Russian simply by being born there, he or she gets to decide what being "Russian" actually means. Does it mean thinking your nation is superior to its neighbors, with the right to invade, to kill, to destroy, in order to dominate their land and their people? Or does it mean a deep Russian spirit that celebrates life, that perhaps pushes you out onto the street to protest your crazy government at your own peril—or even to run against this government the way Alexei Navalny did, regardless of the never-ending risks involved?

Navalny was poisoned by Putin's cronies because his liberalism posed such a danger to Putin's rules as it woke up some of the Russian citizens asleep in a dictatorship for years. Navalny survived this poisoning and recuperated in Europe. He returned to Russia only to be jailed upon entry, to be found guilty on made-up charges that will keep him imprisoned for as long as those who rule by oppression stay in power.

Yet even in the face of danger and threat and risk, we each get to choose who we are, who we will be, how we will define ourselves.

More Choice

I believe the day will dawn when the beauty of each person, of each people, will come to the forefront, no matter how hidden it may seem at the moment. Perhaps Russians will be defined by their passion, Americans by their empathy, Ukrainians by their courage, and on and on and on, until we are all defined by our collective humanity and goodness—citizens of the world.

In the meantime, we can follow Zelenskyy's creed and judge people not by where they're from or what language they speak, but by how they behave in the world, how they *be*. Or we can even choose not to judge them at all—to see the divinity behind their sham.

And we each can present ourselves in a way we can be proud of, regardless of what labels have been given to us by others—or by our own lost selves. In fact, we get to discard any or all of the labels if we feel like it.

Remember: You can let go of the compulsion to be who you've been told you are—to be who you think you're *supposed* to be. Instead, be the You underneath all that. Find that You, define it. As Zelenskyy said, it is a right given to us by God.

2

Anybody Can

I am not a politician. I am just a simple person who has come to break down this system.

—*Zelenskyy, during a 2019 debate prior to his being elected president of Ukraine*

What do you think determines our abilities in life?

Natural-born talent, obviously. And grit, hard work, discipline.

But also, if you listen to extraordinary masters—say, Michael Jordan, who's as superhuman as they come, right?—you realize that at some point in their lives, whether stemming from external encouragement or from an inner knowing, they developed a confidence that went far beyond that of the average person. They mentally eviscerated the idea of limits.

Easier said than done, you may think—that's what I used to think too.

Whatever It Takes

As a twentysomething struggling actress, I was hell-bent on erasing any remnants of a Russian accent I might have had. I took lessons with a renowned speech coach in New York who, in addition to ridding me of the accent, regaled me with stories of Hollywood stars. He told me how, working on audition lines with a very young Julia Roberts—before *Pretty Woman*, before she was iconic throughout the world—she'd been strikingly confident in her abilities and upcoming success, and that once, she looked straight at him and said, "I am Julia Roberts," with a conviction that floored him. In other words, before becoming *the* Julia Roberts that she is to the world, she already was an icon to herself.

Not everyone wants or needs to be an icon, of course, but self-belief is always necessary to go beyond what's expected. My own dad, excited to leave *Sovok* (a nickname for the Soviet Union) for America, decided he would be all right no matter what. Unlike many fellow émigrés who understandably suffered from doubt and anxiety in the grueling months of immigration, my father had confidence that served as fuel. "I'll sweep the streets," he said. "I'll do whatever it takes." In Italy, he used a dictionary to communicate with locals, getting us kids free rides at an amusement park, sneaking us in to watch the circus, and obtaining armloads of overripe unsold fruit from a grocery store—even as the store's guard dog loudly protested this arrangement. Upon coming to the States he wasted no time, making endless calls to companies from a pay phone, listing some immigration worker as his reference. He found work in a matter of weeks, which had been unheard of.

My dad's confidence, like Zelenskyy's, made all the difference during one of the most demanding times in his life. But hey, they're both Ukrainian, right? Though we can all be "a little Ukrainian."

And speaking of dads, how about Richard Williams, aka "King Richard," who decided before they were even born that his daughters Venus and Serena would overcome poverty and become tennis stars? And how about Liz Murray, who attended Harvard despite having been homeless, parentless, sometimes foodless in her high school years?

As much as it is human to flounder in our confidence, based on the seasons, on the opinions of others, on our own doubts and demons, there are tons of examples of those who've overcome all odds. And people who've done this, who've achieved greatness—whatever their arena—usually discovered and committed to their limitlessness before the world confirmed it for them, before they went from "homeless to Harvard," or became a superstar, or an employed immigrant, or President Zelenskyy.

As Ze asked his citizens when he was first elected, "Remember the Iceland soccer team at the European Championship, when a dentist, a director, a pilot, a student, and a cleaner defended their country's honor? No one believed they could do it, but they did it!

"And this should be precisely our path," he explained. "We must become the Icelanders in soccer, the Israelis in the defense of their native land, the Japanese in technology, and the Swiss in the ability to live with each other in harmony, despite all the differences."

He was urging Ukrainians to see past limits—just as he had done himself.

Slava Ukraini (Glory to Ukraine)

Prior to Russia's full-scale war in Ukraine, the world knew little of the incredible gusto and leadership of our man Zelenskyy; I'd go as far as to say he was treated without respect, as was his country. He had to eat a lot of poop, for lack of a better phrase. He was but a pawn within the game of American politics during the Trump era, for instance, visibly uncomfortable in that role (see the next chapter). And there was that time in 2020 when Secretary of State Mike Pompeo infamously yelled at a reporter, "You think Americans care about Ukraine?"

But Zelenskyy wanted Americans to care about Ukraine. Why wouldn't we care about Europe's biggest country, with its fertile land, its proud production of wheat, its yearning for freedom and peace? In fact, much of the world hadn't realized how imperative it was for us to care until it was almost too late. But—thanks in large part to Ze—the emphasis here falls on the "almost" part.

Ukraine, even as it was on fire, showed us a collective spirit so strong it reminded us of our own. Because we all have it within us somewhere. And Ze masterfully brought this admirable spirit onto the world stage.

Still, even as Ukraine's mouthpiece during the many months of fighting, Zelenskyy had to walk a fine line: he had to ask for support; ask for weapons from the rest of the free world without groveling or losing his self-assuredness, as well as his assuredness in the goodness and the power of his country. That is exactly what he did, though—he walked that fine line, as if effortlessly, because his dignity and pride did not depend on external validation. And his people— his army and his citizens—were infused with a belief in Ukraine that superseded uncertainty. Believing in themselves and their nation—and their president—they tapped into an inner power that allowed them to be the David to Russia's Goliath.

"The spirits of our army are high," Zelenskyy's former press secretary Iuliia Mendel told WBUR early on in the war. "Our army is going to stand against the enemy.

"I am proud," she said. "People here on the ground, they are very proud that they have these defenders standing against [the] furious Russian army."

And in a video address half a year into the war, Zelenskyy continued to remind folks how far they've come: "On February 24 we were told: you have no chance. On August 24 we say, 'Happy Independence Day, Ukraine.' During these six months we changed history, changed the world, and changed ourselves.

"We believe in ourselves! We believe in Ukraine!" he proclaimed.

And so it was.

Patience as Self-Love

One of the big blocks to our success and fulfillment these days is impatience. Many of us are products of our era of instant gratification, which has grown ever more instant. If we have dreams, goals, visions, we want their manifestation yesterday—how could we not?

The problem is, if we don't see our dreams come to fruition fast enough, we lose hope or even throw in the towel.

But here's the thing: faith in our own abilities, in our limitlessness, is a timeless affair—it's a constant. If we keep the faith regardless of what is or isn't happening and we keep going, eventually, the limitlessness triumphs. That is what shaped the life of Volodymyr Zelenskyy, long before any of us knew who he was.

As a young Jewish boy from an educated family in Ukraine—his father was a professor of computer science, his mother an engineer—Zelenskyy dreamed of performing, of being a star. Regardless of his family's commitment to education, he was pulled toward the arts. But what I've realized, what I suspect Zelenskyy grasped all along, is that creativity is always at our disposal, and as much as it needs attention to flourish, it also benefits from an indestructible will.

Coming of age in the steel town of Kryvyy Rih, Zelenskyy faced his share of obstacles. For one, he was navigating a Soviet regime that was crumbling. The country's instability brewed violence and street gangs all over the faltering USSR; like most youngsters, he was affected. When he took up playing guitar as a teen, for instance, thugs smashed his instrument to pieces. He'd been playing some rock 'n' roll in an underpass when it happened; as he told his friends, "I guess Kryvyy Rih isn't ready for us yet." He shrugged off the incident and continued on his path to eventual stardom.

To appease the trepidation of his parents, who wanted stability for him as most parents do, Zelenskyy attained a law degree—which I'm sure is of use to him in his current position, or at least the ability to cram complex information is of use. But he also kept pursuing his passion for comedy, performing with his local troupe, including on television (he never actually worked as a lawyer). Still, full success took time—years, in fact, before he found footing in an industry that's competitive regardless of which country you're in. It was a long while before he became a household name.

Later, when he decided to run for president, some members of the Jewish community felt that he shouldn't, fearing his rise to power would attract anti-Semitism. The thing is, though, fear never deterred our hero (see chapter 10). For when you don't believe in limits, nothing can deter you.

*　　*　　*

Zelensky's faith in himself is what propelled him forward in life. First he charted an unstoppable path to comedic stardom, and then . . . well, we know what happened from there. It is this persistence, this boundlessness of his that initially captivated me. When I was on set of *Love in the Big City*, for example, Zelenskyy was one of three key stars in the film and, in fact, it was his first time headlining a major movie. A decade later, he was president of his nation.

How is that possible? I kept thinking.

Watching him along with the rest of the world, I realized his unwillingness to heed limits was key. It spilled over from his belief in self to his belief that "everything is possible"—which is what he told former Soviet countries upon winning the Ukrainian election. These former Soviet republics, like my birthplace of Latvia—well, there's plenty of cynicism to go around there, and understandably so. People had suffered for generations under an oppressive regime, and the kind of corruption we all lived with—it stays with you. Yet, Zelenskyy said, "To all the countries of the former Soviet Union, look at us . . . everything is possible," and his actions kept showing us the truth of his words.

"There are no shackles that can bind our free spirit," Ze told his people in a nightly video address in May.

There are no limits when you realize *you're* limitless.

The Extraordinary Ordinary

What is so incredible about our man Volodymyr is that his belief in himself stems not from seeing himself as special, but from seeing himself as ordinary and from knowing there is great power in this ordinariness. His belief, in other words, is in the abilities of each ordinary individual.

"Each of us is the president now," he said in his inaugural address. "Every one of us is the leader of our time," he told the *Time* 100 Gala. And this is a belief system, a celebration of the power of the ordinary, that differs greatly from the constraints most of us have bought into. For from the time we are born, limits are placed upon us left and right: "Don't go there, don't touch that," we are told. "Stop, you can't, *no!*"

Obviously, some boundaries are necessary as we begin to navigate the world—they're meant to keep us safe, to help us stay alive. However, as we grow, these boundaries quickly morph from ones of safety to those of limited beliefs.

"It's not possible to make a living creatively," for instance, is a stubborn belief many of us "starving artists" have buried deep within us, having never known anyone who went after their dreams and "made it."

"You can't prosper if you're honest," we repeat to ourselves and to one another. "You can't be a good person and be wealthy." "You can't buck the system."

Somehow, though, Volodymyr Zelenskyy, born under the very same limit-inducing regime as millions of us were, saw beyond these imposed restrictions (ones that—let's be honest—can be found in all cultures). He gleaned a reality in which, he, "an ordinary person," as he called himself, could rise up and make a difference.

Limitless Beings

The question beckons then, can you too rise up to the ranks of greatness? Can you too lead impeccably, triumph under pressure, change what's possible?

Why not, right? *What's stopping you?!*

Wait . . . don't answer that question. There are a gazillion excuses we can each conjure of what can get in the way of our Inner Zelenskyy. Let's skip this line of thinking for now, and just fast-forward to the *Yes*.

Yes, you can, in fact, tap into your own invincibility—and this I say with complete certainty. Yes, you are ordinary and yes, you are extraordinary, and it is up to you to embrace the former and realize the latter. As Volodymyr Zelenskyy has taught us, each one of us is, in fact, our own president; each of us is our own leader.

And so it is always the right time to stop doubting our greatness and/or begging the world to recognize it. Let's find it within ourselves, instead, on our own, and the world will follow suit. . . . And sometimes it won't. But we can believe in ourselves regardless. It is this belief that will carry us through failure and success alike, just like it carries President Zelenskyy.

Ze's approval ratings were quite low before the full-scale war began—well, first they were high, then they were low—and yet most Ukrainians were incredibly grateful for his leadership in their darkest hour, as they recognized the assuredness, the faith, the steadfastness he carried within him all along. His citizens looked to *him* for guidance and reinforcement when their very lives were at stake—they'd end their days by watching his nightly addresses, feeling soothed by him, being enlivened by his faith. Of course, he is not perfect, nor does he pretend to be. "A regular human," is what he's called himself time and time again. Still, it is his faith and confidence in his ordinary self—an ordinary self without limits—that gets him through any situation.

Since, as Zelenskyy says, we are each a leader in our own right, it us on us to grow our belief and our confidence in ourselves, in our abilities, in our projects. It is on us to carry ourselves as the limitless beings we are.

As the famous Henry Ford quote goes, "Whether you think you can or you can't, you are right." Let us believe then that we can!

And this belief in oneself need not be a grand operation, by the way—dominating a sport or the box office, or leading a country—but, rather, as Zelenskyy has shown us, it all begins with the acceptance and the love of our very ordinariness. That is how he stands out from both regular folks and from exceptional figures: he embraces being "a simple person" *and* he believes in his ability "to break down this system."

He reminds us that an ordinary person can absolutely achieve great things, if only they believe that they can. And they get to define these "great things" however they wish.

So how about you? What is your "great thing(s)" that you want to achieve or become or create? Aim far, dream beyond the limits—even of your own mind.

Remember, in the words of Volodymyr Zelenskyy: "Everything is possible."

3

How May I Serve?

> "I want people to take me as I am, a regular human,"
> *Zelenskyy said in a CNN interview in April 2022.*
> "Definitely not a hero."

How curious is it that the world's foremost hero says he wants people to see him as "definitely *not* a hero"? How paradoxical that a person who has the utmost belief in himself does not see himself as more special than anyone else?

Or perhaps it's not surprising at all that Ze thinks this way, but rather, it is the very mindset of a heroic person, of a fine leader, of a sage, even: humility.

As the Tao Te Ching says (that's the ancient spiritual philosophy that serves as an anchor for many a searcher): "The sage puts himself last, and so ends up first." And "the highest virtue is not virtuous; therefore it truly has virtue." A heroic person does not think about their own heroism; they simply do what needs to be done. They act in accordance with their moral clarity, their Inner Zelenskyy, if you will. And they see this as absolutely ordinary.

As we spoke of in the past chapter, Zelenskyy's power comes from a limitlessness that's based in his own ordinariness. Yes, he believes in himself greatly *and* he believes in the honor of his people. He doesn't see what he's achieved in life as making him better than anyone else. "We are all ordinary people," remember?

Of course, our man is sure of his own capabilities—he had faith in his strength as a performer long before he became famous, for one—but he doesn't view these capabilities as a bigger deal than anyone else's. Since the beginning of the war, he has thanked countless workers and professionals for their contribution to his country in the face of violence. And his gratitude and respect for all of these people was palpable. Being their great spokesperson and their leader during a difficult time was only natural for him. He fulfilled his role just as they fulfilled theirs.

Dyakuyu (Thank You)

"Thank you for the tens of thousands of second birthdays you gave to our military, our civilians, our Ukrainian children," Zelenskyy told his nation's doctors in June 2022, with eyes full of emotion. "Thank you for saving lives . . ." he said, "lives—the most precious thing."

And he thanked Ukraine's farmers, "who defended their communities even with bare hands . . . Who, despite the war, ensured a sowing campaign." He said, "The whole world has seen who Ukrainian farmers really are, and what the work of our agricultural sector is worth," referring to their wheat exports having been blocked by Russia, and without which the world's precarious food security became endangered.

"Only thanks to journalists we managed to unite the world, and we united ourselves within our state," Zelenskyy said in May 2022. He expressed gratitude to his national soccer team for "two hours of happiness" when it won its World Cup semifinal against Scotland—despite preparation that was very much complicated by the war. "There are times when you don't need many words!" he wrote. "Pride is enough! Simply thanks to you guys!"

Months later, when the Ukraine women's national team won gold at the 44th Chess Olympiad in India, "The whole country is proud of your result," Ze posted. "Thank you for such an important victory and the Ukrainian flag on the highest step of the pedestal!" And he again praised the capability of his people when Oleksandr Usyk defended the world heavyweight title—Usyk himself saying that he was boxing for his whole country and, really, for half the world. When he won, Zelenskyy posted "Difficult, but so important and necessary VICTORY!"

Here's the thing: Zelenskyy's pride is a collective pride—it's a pride on behalf of his entire nation, which banded together at a crucial time. As he told CNN's Jake Tapper, the strength of everyday Ukrainians gives him all the inspiration he needs—from citizens having to hide in cellars for months, to those on the front lines, and everyone in between. "I believe our people are genuine and unique," he said, "and I just can't afford to be worse than them."

With a pride born of this understanding, only humility is possible. And with humility intact, one can never become an obnoxious Icarus, no matter how important or famous one gets.

And so our hero does not see himself as such. He does not fall into the trap of ego that so many succumb to at their height, plummeting to the ground in a tragic downward spiral. Our guy knows better. He knows his success depends on talents given to him at birth. He was a born performer, speaker, entertainer, and in Ukraine's most dire moment, those are the abilities he leaned on to lead it and to capture the world's attention. He doesn't think he's special because of his gifts, he just uses them to fulfill his duty. And so he is anchored in his true self, not falling prey to that overinflated ego in the way of countless other politicians across the globe. It is clear who Zelenskyy is serving here . . . remember the name of his show and then his political party?

Servant of the People.

Humility through Service

Servant leadership, the humblest of leadership styles, has appeared in one form or another since the beginning of humankind. It is the type of leadership purported by the Tao Te Ching, for one—which roughly translates as "the

Way of Integrity." "Serve the needs of others and all your own needs will be fulfilled," the Tao has suggested since the sixth century BC. And yet even in the United States of America, it was power-centered authoritarian leadership that was most prominent within companies—not to mention that it was the way many countries were (and continue to be) governed across the globe.

In 1970, Robert K. Greenleaf, an American who had spent decades researching the then-standard authoritarian structure in US institutions, wrote the essay "The Servant as Leader" about an alternative approach. He later penned *The Essentials of Servant Leadership*, introducing the phrase and influencing leadership education for decades to come. "The servant-leader is servant first," he taught. "It begins with a natural feeling that one wants to serve." He espoused that a servant-leader was in sharp contrast to someone who was a leader first, hungry for power and/or influence. A servant-leader instead put his focus on the growth and well-being of people and communities, sharing power with them, prioritizing their needs, and helping them perform their best.

Robert K. Greenleaf may not have known Volodymyr Zelenskyy—and Zelenskyy may not have heard of Robert K. Greenleaf—but the person he described in his philosophy was exactly the kind of leader Zelenskyy has become. And our servant-leader or "Servant of the People" is as humble a trailblazer as the world has ever seen.

"I'm not iconic, I think Ukraine is iconic," he told CNN when he was praised for his wartime response. Because— recall his mindset: he is simply doing his duty.

He laid it all out in his inaugural address in 2019: "All

my life I tried to do all I could so that Ukrainians laughed," he said. "That was my mission. Now I will do all I can so that Ukrainians at least do not cry anymore."

And so it was.

Eat Humble Pirozhki

How do we cultivate a mindset of humility?

First we need to understand it.

Humility is one of those qualities that can be perceived as weakness or lack of ambition, I'm afraid, especially in our "What's in it for me?" era. So let us dissect what humility is exactly by looking at the example Zelenskyy has laid before us: his love of life, his commitment, his gratitude.

Ze is a person who has full faith and confidence, not just in himself, as we've seen, but also in the fact that good will triumph over evil—he has said as much numerous times since darkness enveloped his land. Why would he seek aggrandizement, then, when his beliefs are so pure? What he's shown us is that purity and simplicity are, in fact, humility—the humble and beautiful experience of being a human in the world. And one enjoyable aspect of being human that he's managed to hold on to is humor.

When actor Ben Stiller visited Kyiv as a UN goodwill ambassador in June 2022, he lavished Ze with praise—too much praise ("It's too much for me," Zelenskyy had answered, slightly uncomfortable). But Stiller cutely gushed "You're my hero. You're amazing. You quit a great acting career for this." To which our man replied, "Not as great as yours," with a smile. And, sense of humor intact, Ze moved on with the work of advocating for his land.

Of course, self-deprecation has been used by comedians since the birth of comedy. It is a great, entertaining reminder that we are but human, flawed, and not as amazing as we may seem or pretend to be. And it's a tool that in Zelenskyy's case is a sign of modesty and of truth: yes, he is sometimes self-deprecating, and yes, he means it. And he toggles humor with utmost seriousness like a pro.

The leaders of old tended to stay on brand—like Winston Churchill, who Ze has often been compared to, and who sure knew a thing or two about branding. Churchill was inspirational. Firm, powerful, confident, world-changing. But would he wave off praise and deflect it with jokes? Would he "Who, me?" his admirers like an old friend?

It is Zelenskyy's knack for being both Churchill– *and* Ben Stiller–like that makes him so unique. It is his toggling ability that makes him so relatable.

Not a Hero

In April 2022 when journalist Jake Tapper asked Zelenskyy how he would want to be remembered—if, in fact, he did not make it through the war—he answered, "[As] a human being that loved life to the fullest, and loved his family, and loved his motherland. Definitely not as a hero," he added.

"I want people to take me as I am—a regular human."

Ze has demonstrated that humility and humanity are one: the love of it all—of existence and of others. In appreciating life, he is naturally humble. In appreciating his people, he wants to help them flourish; he is naturally a servant-leader.

We can all learn to practice this humble form of leadership in our jobs and in our homes: a governance based in service. I mean, most parents feel like servants to their children anyway, right? And sometimes, we resent it. In dissecting the humble leadership style of our Ze, though, perhaps we can occupy our roles more fully, more readily—whether within families or in communities and organizations. Perhaps we are all here to simply serve one another. When we realize this, we can be both humble in our wins and gracious in our losses. "What difference between yes and no?" the Tao Te Ching asks, "What difference between success and failure?"

Instead, *How may I serve?* is the spiritual question we are learning to ask. *How may I serve?*

Go deep, then, and figure out your role—or ask that service question—then carry it out, over and over again. Do that and you'll become successful—or at least, you'll become actualized (one and the same, in my opinion). You'll become the hero of your own life . . . or definitely *not* a hero, as Zelenskyy would say.

4

Know Your Purpose/ Know Your Audience

"Very often people ask who is Zelenskyy's speech-writer," *Dasha Zarivna, a communications adviser, told* Time *magazine in April 2022.* "The main one is him. He works on every line."

When someone so naturally inhabits the very life they were born to lead, magic happens. When this person fulfills their raison d'être, their dharma, their soul's purpose, it is incomparable to anyone or anything else, really. No one had ever done exactly what they're doing, because this exact doing—and being—of theirs is theirs and theirs alone.

Volodymyr Zelenskyy is just such a person—someone who fully inhabits his purpose.

This lovable actor/comedian/entertainer turned astute wartime leader . . . well . . . to say he's been fulfilling his dharma is to state the obvious. Which is why there is no one else like Zelenskyy (or, say, like Oprah Winfrey, or like the Vietnamese Buddhist monk Thích Nhất Hạnh). People like that are in a category all their own. And Ze understands his category—his unique purpose in this exact moment in time—naturally and wholly. That is what makes him so good at his job.

Dharma

As soon as Russia launched its war on Ukraine, Ze innately understood what his country needed of him. He knew that his leadership and strength in the face of possible annihilation was of the utmost importance, and so he put it ahead of his own safety, even. He also knew he had to tirelessly speak up for Ukraine—for its beauty, its valor, its struggle, and its importance to Europe and to the world as a whole. And so he represented his nation, drawing a vivid picture of what it was going through around the clock—and he kept on telling us, never letting up.

Perhaps most significantly, Volodymyr Zelenskyy understood that to get his message to land, he had to speak directly to each audience that was listening to him. He had to connect with them on a greater level than he'd ever connected with anyone. And luckily he knew *how* to do that—after all, he'd already won an unlikely presidency.

Historic Empathy

When Zelenskyy ran for president of Ukraine in 2019, he tapped directly into the discontent and the fed-upness the Ukrainian people felt toward their representatives to date. He felt that same fed-upness, himself; he had long used it as fodder in his comedy routines and as the basis of the very sitcom that led him to seek the real-life position of "Servant of the People." It was his ability to connect deeply to what the Ukrainian people were feeling that equaled his success in both entertainment and in politics—a discontent we can easily understand when we look at the country's fraught recent history. . . .

After the fall of the Soviet Union in 1991, Ukraine continued to flounder under officials who bent to Putin's will, rather than representing the people's will—the people's desire to move forward as a nation, to westernize their economy, and to join the European Union—to be fully free, rather than tethered to Russia.

In 2014, in what became known as the Revolution of Dignity (or the Euro-Maidan Revolution), mass protests in Kyiv—including deadly clashes with security forces—toppled the reign of Viktor Yanukovych, the Putin ally in charge. Yanukovych, conceding to Moscow's request, had refused to sign an association agreement with the European Union that was very much desired by Ukrainians. When thousands of protesters took control of central Kyiv, Yanukovych fled the city and an interim government was formed.

Putin responded to Ukraine's disposal of his supporter—to the people's struggle to fully free themselves of Russia's reins—by annexing Crimea and by sending troops into the east of the country, which soon turned into the war in Donbas. It was this war, this struggle that Zelenskyy inherited.

Within Ukraine there were also internal problems to deal with. Even as citizens brought down Putin's puppet president—even as some lost their lives for this—corruption ran rampant under Zelenskyy's predecessor, the prominent oligarch Petro Poroshenko.

"In my opinion, an oligarch cannot be president," Ze had said when he ran against him. "A president needs to come from the people." And because he had his finger on the pulse of the people, because he was one of them, the people spoke, granting him a landslide victory of over 73 percent.

Zelenskyy empathized with fellow citizens so fully, one might say he intuitively understood what they needed. He got how pissed off they were, having risked so much for Ukraine's shot at self-determination, only to put up with bullsh*t from its newer government. As he told the incumbent during a 2019 presidential debate, "I am not your opponent, Pyotr Alexeyevich [Poroshenko], I am your sentence."

In understanding what his people wanted, Ze wanted it for them. He had enjoyed the fruits of his own hard work in the entertainment field and he yearned for everyone in his nation to have that kind of opportunity. "We will build the country of other opportunities," he said upon being elected, instead of "the opportunities to bribe, steal, and pluck resources" that the "pompous system politicians" had created up until then. He vowed to establish a framework "where all are equal before the law and where all the rules are honest and transparent, the same for everyone."

"This is our common dream," he said, referring to Ukraine's desire to westernize and to flourish, while simultaneously remembering those protecting Ukrainian interests on the front lines. "I will do everything I can to make you feel respect," he told Ukrainian troops, naming decent salaries and living conditions as a must for soldiers and their families. "We are not the ones who have started this war," he said. "But we are the ones who have to finish it."

By marrying patriotism to the dire need for change and restructuring, Zelenskyy won over the country he was destined to lead through darkness. And his ability to connect with those he wanted to influence proved a great boon to the country's very survival.

Hearts and Minds

Representing his nation on a global stage required all of Ze's gifts and experience to date: winning the hearts and minds of non-Ukrainians by showing them that Ukraine's struggle was, in fact, their own. In fulfilling this role, he brought an uncanny level of insight and connection that caused leaders—and also thousands upon thousands of civilians—to think about the plight of Ukraine.

As Ukraine's mouthpiece, Zelenskyy channeled the dignity of the underdog, while meeting listeners exactly where they were—from tailoring his speeches to one government at a time, to chatting with celebrities like Ashton Kutcher and Mila Kunis (who raised millions of dollars for Ukraine). Knowing how to present his message to different people was key to his success—his ability to persuade nations and organizations to dedicate significant funds, resources, and attention to his cause.

"For us, such visits of famous people are extremely valuable," he said when actress Jessica Chastain met with him in Kyiv. "Thanks to this, the world will hear, know, and understand the truth about what is happening in our country even more. Thanks for the support!"

Sensing exactly how to reach people on an emotional level was Zelenskyy's superpower.

"It's not a Berlin Wall," he told German legislators at the onset of the war, "it is a wall in central Europe between freedom and bondage and this wall is growing bigger with every bomb" dropped on Ukraine.

And to the British parliament he said, "We do not want to lose what we have, what is ours. . . . Just the same way you once didn't want to lose your country when the Nazis started to fight. . . . We will fight until the end, at sea, in the air. We will continue fighting for our land," he added, echoing Winston Churchill's famous World War II speech. And he invoked Shakespeare: "To be or not to be," saying that question could certainly apply to Ukraine. "It's definitely yes, to be."

He again spoke brazenly and powerfully to American legislators. "Remember Pearl Harbor, the terrible morning of

December 7, 1941, when your sky was black from the planes attacking you," Zelenskyy appealed to Congress. "Just remember it. . . . Remember September 11, a terrible day in 2001, when evil tried to turn your cities—independent territories—into battlefields." He then added, "Our country experiences the same every day, right now, at this moment—every night for three weeks now."

The Power of Creativity

Zelenskyy's ability to align his message to the ethos of each nation was key not only to the standing ovations, but more important, to the support that poured in. And he used that same technique when speaking with actors and musicians and, even, advertisers—virtually commanding the room, always sporting his military fatigues and his unshaven exhaustion.

"Our musicians wear body armor instead of tuxedos. They sing to the wounded in hospitals—even to those who can't hear them," he said at the 2022 Grammys. "But the music will break through anyway. We defend our freedom to live, to love, to sound."

"It's necessary for cinema not to be silent," he pronounced at the Cannes Film Festival. "I say to everyone who hears me: Do not despair. Hatred will eventually disappear and," he added, echoing the work of Charlie Chaplin, "dictators will die."

"The power of human creativity is greater than the power of a nuclear state that is stuck in the past," he told those gathered at the Cannes Lions advertising festival—and he certainly planned to prove it.

Whomever he was speaking to, he never missed the chance to personalize his message. And as his communications adviser Dasha Zarivna explained to *Time* magazine, Zelenskyy was his own main speechwriter—he, himself, worked on every line.

"The power of human creativity is greater than the power of a nuclear state," he had proclaimed.

And so it was.

Information Wars

At the very onset of the war, Zelenskyy got to work, combining an aggressive meeting schedule with his frequent speeches, press conferences and, also, nightly video addresses to his citizens.

The Ukrainian president understood the importance of the information war, and combated Russia's propaganda by speaking openly and vulnerably, especially to his own people—sometimes switching from Ukrainian to Russian in case citizens of Russia would hear him as well. Just as he combined gratitude with bold requests for more help when communicating with other governments, he struck a balance for his hometown audience. He always managed to blend his faith in Ukraine with the truth of the destruction it was facing.

Basically, he'd say it like it was, but in the same breath, he'd offer hope and commend Ukraine's bravery, and he would set an example of perseverance. Plus, he used the best modern tool to create intimacy and immediacy—social media.

"Good evening to you all," Zelenskyy spoke from the heart of Kyiv in a now-famous video he posted on the second day of war. "The head of government is here. The head of the president's office is here. Prime Minister Shmyhal is here. Adviser Podoliak is here. The president is here. Our soldiers are here. Our citizens are here. We are all defending our independence—our country—and it will stay that way. Glory to the men and women defending us. Glory to Ukraine. Glory to the heroes."

For days, then weeks, then months, he posted videos that echoed that most famous one—even reprising it on the hundredth day of war. Over and over, he showed his people that he was still there, still working as hard as ever to secure Ukraine's future, and he instilled confidence that he—and they—would keep defending their land for as long as it took.

While Russia twisted the reality of its "special military operation" to its citizens, downplaying, ignoring, lying about the atrocities it had unleashed against Ukrainian civilians—as well as about its own losses, thousands upon thousands of soldiers—Zelenskyy always spoke openly about Ukraine's grave situation, paying homage to every life lost.

While Putin and Co. tightened the flow of information in their country, punishing with draconian sentences those who spoke out against the war, Zelenskyy opted for as much transparency as he could muster.

As ruler of Russia, which is what Putin supposedly

wanted to be called, he answered to no one. As Servant of the People, Zelenskyy reported to them constantly, letting them know exactly what he was doing on their behalf, whom he was talking to, and what his government was working on.

This picture of repression versus freedom couldn't be more stark. But it just so happens, there's no better weapon in an information war than respecting your audience.

Tips from Ze

Humans are storytelling machines. It is an ability that is one of our greatest assets when presenting ourselves to others, when wanting anything from anyone, when working to accomplish our goals and dreams. And so it's an asset worth honing, as Zelenskyy had done his entire adult life, whether through performance or public speaking.

Amid his other impressive qualities, Zelenskyy is a master storyteller—which is the attribute that helped us pay attention to him in the first place. And in looking at his advanced ability to communicate, we too can become better communicators. So let's get to it.

- As Ze has demonstrated, we build trust with people through transparency and through a direct, no-BS style of communication. Be ballsy, be honest, be clear.
- Also, find a common thread with those you're talking to; talk specifically to them, just like he did with every

audience. Because when others see themselves in you, their support is that much more likely.

- Combine your passion for your cause with humility, and support it with facts to prove your point. Zelenskyy sometimes bolstered his speeches with videos of the suffering Russia was unleashing in Ukraine—those facts, that heartbreak of innocent civilians, were unignorable.

- Be specific in your ask, keeping your primary—and perhaps secondary—objective at the forefront. When Zelenskyy first spoke with Congress, he said, "Is this a lot to ask for, to create a no-fly zone over Ukraine to save people?" Knowing that the Biden administration was unwilling to do this, having already called it a recipe for World War III, Ze added, "If this is too much to ask, we offer an alternative." And he brought up the defense systems his nation needed to protect itself.

- Make your listeners feel valued. Ze never missed an opportunity to thank his helpers—and not just the countries that helped Ukraine, but the citizens of those countries. He acknowledged his European and American partners almost daily, even as he asked for more assistance. He understood that gratitude was the key to bringing in more of what you were grateful for.

- Lastly, remember, whether speaking publicly or one-on-one, while you are not Zelenskyy, you are You—a unique person with your own experiences and strengths. You can be inspired by Ze, but you need not (actually, you can't) be him. What you can do best is be your unique and authentic self.

5

Just Be Real

I do not try to play a role. I feel good being myself and saying what I think.

—In an interview with the Guardian *on March 7, 2020, shortly after President Trump's impeachment. Trump was accused of trying to bribe Zelenskyy by promising to greatly help Ukraine if Zelenskyy's people would dig up dirt on Joe Biden's son, Hunter, who had done business in the region. Trump had allegedly held up Ukraine's military aid package in order to pressure an investigation of the younger Biden.*

Being real, being yourself is the optimal choice in life—we all know this intuitively. It is freeing, empowering, honest.

Yet this realness can also feel difficult and burdensome, when who you are or what you do doesn't fall into the popular line of being and doing things—when it just doesn't fit, when you don't fit.

So how do we bridge the disparity?

Well, many of us cower to the pressure around us. We simply (not so simply) veer away from our core selves.

And yet there have always been people like Volodymyr Zelenskyy, for whom it's easier to take the criticism, to take the heat, than to *not* be real. Because, regardless of anyone else's reaction, "I feel good being myself," as he put it.

The Irony of Fate

In his 2020 talk with the *Guardian*, Zelenskyy did not deny the compliments he had paid US president Donald Trump during their infamous July 2019 phone conversation—the very phone call whose transcript became the focus of Trump's first impeachment. Zelenskyy had not come out looking good from that call, placating the American president with praise (i.e., "You're a great teacher for us") while pussyfooting around his persistent request to investigate Hunter Biden.

Zelenskyy's critics accused him of kissing up to Trump. Which, objectively, he did, if you read the transcript. Yet, as he explained to the *Guardian*, the compliments he'd paid our polarizing president came from a genuine place—as did his promise to run only honest investigations.

Ze revealed that Trump's 2016 presidential win was significant to him in that it showed him how a nonpolitical person can alter the political game. "And in this, he really was an example of how you can win without using the standard format," he said. Trump's unusual victory inspired him. It gave him confidence to go for it himself in *his* homeland, which he did by using everything he had under his belt—not the least of which was authenticity.

"I do not try to play a role," he'd said. "I feel good being myself and saying what I think."

Ironic, of course, coming from a lifelong performer—but not any more ironic than a US leader trying to bribe a Ukrainian one after years of America chiding Ukraine for its Soviet-era level of corruption. This was exactly the type of corruption Zelenskyy had hoped to clean up, and he couldn't do it by being anyone other than himself—in all his larger-than-life iterations. And yes, the himself that he was paid compliments to Donald Trump, because he looked for the good, for the *can*, in every situation.

Story Line

When Zelenskyy ran for president of Ukraine, he beat the incumbent, a confectionary billionaire, with an unprecedented share of the vote. In interviews, he had said that unlike the previous Ukrainian president, the oligarch Petro Poroshenko, he'd made every penny he had by using his own talent.

Even as I watch this talent today, on display in his old comedy clips (the bulk of them in Russian), I'm struck by what can be seen only as the hand of fate—the fate in which this man created the literal part of a lifetime: a sitcom where he portrayed a regular guy, a teacher, whose anticorruption speech went viral and got him elected president. This show, *Servant of the People* (which can now be watched with subtitles on Netflix) was like the golden key for our hero. He was so good at this role because it aligned with his own soul.

"I started out making fun of politicians, parodying them, and in so doing, showing what kind of Ukraine I would like to see," Zelenskyy told the *New Yorker*.

He was this humorous everyman with an honest heart, and then he *did* win over his people, and he *was* elected president. Life imitates the art that imitates life. Oh, the seamless story line.

I don't know about you but I'm pretty certain that bigger forces were at play here, as Zelenskyy portrayed a TV role that he was destined to live out in the real world, during a war, no less—a war in which his leadership would win him an Oscar or an Emmy, had it been scripted. But, alas, it was not. It was very real and very tragic, and I'm sure part of him wished it were a script. Still, his country and the world were lucky to have him. Who could have done a better job than this seemingly unlikely "leader of the West," as the media dubbed him?

As Ze's former adviser Igor Novikov explained, "He has a performer's sixth sense of what people want. . . . In a time of crisis, he is a lens that channels the energies of the people into a single beam of light."

It is no wonder, then, that these people saw something

in him even as he got endless flak from critics for his lack of political experience. The people's choice of Zelenskyy as their leader made all the difference in their nation's survival. And what the whole world gets to see in Ze now—what Ukrainians must have glimpsed when they elected him—is his utmost humanity, his realness . . . not to mention his simple brilliance. The emotion in his eyes tells us he is being himself, he is being truthful, he says what he thinks.

Unlike many of his colleagues in the region, Zelenskyy's past did not turn him into an immoral Soviet-style politician. In fact, all the playing he did for a living put him that much more in touch with his own core, with both his strength and his vulnerability—since, often, our best creations stem from our very humanness.

As Zelenskyy had said during his presidential campaign, "You don't need experience to be president. You just have to be a decent human being."

Authentic as a Verb

Where in your life can you stand to be more authentic?

This is not a trick question—more like nutritious borscht for thought.

"I do not try to play a role," Volodymyr Zelenskyy had said, which is amusing, coming from a comedic actor who ran for president. And yet he was being honest. This is why he did become president, and a great one at that. He did so by being himself, by doing the next right thing. Which, of course, doesn't mean he didn't make mistakes. It's just that

in his himself-ness, his simple goodness shone through—
and when you're real like that, you give yourself the best
shot at everything.

Since being real entails dismantling the programming
we've all been imbued with for generations, there's always
another level of veracity to get to, another mask to remove.
Yet Zelenskyy has shown us that it's the very intention to
be authentic, to be oneself, that counts, rather than perfection. He's shown us that truth is a verb—it's being who
you are and saying what you think in this very moment, no
matter how messy, and then adapting to the next moment
as it unfolds.

"Maybe a leader is not supposed to talk like this," Zelenskyy said in several of his wartime videos and interviews,
"but . . ."—fill in the honest blank. By not doing what he
was "supposed" to do, he did truth. And that's exactly how
this Ukrainian president rose to hero status—by rising to
the moment while remaining genuine.

Such honesty is just as much an internal experience as it
is an external one: "I feel good being myself," he had said,
"and saying what I think." Because when you stick to your
deepest authenticity, you don't look outside of yourself for
your next move—the *supposed to*s, the *should*s, the validation. You feel good about being you, the core You that is
infinite; you trust it. It is God, Source Energy, the Tao that
you then allow to come through you. . . . At least that's the
way I see it. In my view, Zelenskyy has channeled God energy in his leadership.

An Audit

How many of us, do you think, are ready to make a commitment to being authentic? At least more of the time. How much of our protective, egoic covering are we ready to chuck?

It may just be that simple: a commitment to being real. Because even for a heroic person like Zelenskyy, it becomes easy (or easier) to do the right thing when being true plainly becomes a way of being.

So I encourage you to do an audit of yourself and of your own life to see what layers of inauthenticity you're ready to peel—without judgment or blame or shame—simply an honest assessment. You can start by paying attention to all the times you do what you're *supposed* to instead of what you're pulled to do. Start observing this tug-of-war within you so that when you're ready, you can begin choosing differently.

Maybe your *supposed-to*s are keeping you from your passion or are sapping you of the energy you need to better care for yourself and your loved ones. Maybe they're holding you back from being a bolder, brighter version of yourself.

Maybe your inauthenticity lies in the icky thread that runs through some relationships—all of the things said behind each other's backs, all of the things left unsaid. Or it's the job you go to every morning, which you hate but keep because dependents and mortgage and, after all, the drink at the end of the day melts away your distaste. And perhaps the steps to become more honest in your life will be incremental at first: an unfilled silence, an open conversation with your spouse, a late night alone in a hard chair.

As Zelenskyy has demonstrated, when you treat truth as a verb, it'll get that much easier to be it, moment by moment. And then, no matter what is crumbling or chaosing around you, you're able to do the right thing with less struggle—even when it's the hardest thing.

6

Speak Truth to Everything

"The truth will defeat any lies. . . . It's only a matter of time," Zelenskyy said in an April 2022 video address to his people. He added, "This is about who can speak truthfully, both with his people and with the whole world."

"The clown president," as Volodymyr Zelenskyy had been called, may seem like an oxymoron, or some sort of satire at best. Maybe it's ludicrous, even. Yet if we look at the basis of humor, of art, of entertainment—and of decent government (another oxymoron?)—it all begins to make sense. Because it is truth, actually, that's at the heart of all great art and all great comedy—and Zelenskyy was a damn good comic.

Ze's performances were pee-in-your-pants funny, including that famous skit in which he seemingly plays the piano with his genitals. And you might think, how could the silliness of sketch comedy, or of any performance art for that matter, morph into solid leadership? His critics have been asking that question since he came to power. Well, the answer became clear during his toughest days.

The answer is simply: truth.

For truth *is* simple and yet it evades us constantly. From our leaders to those closest to us, it can be hard to come by. But it is one of Zelenskyy's main tools—speak truth, seek truth—and it's one that he committed to long before he became president.

Theater

Most actors are taught—or figure out experientially—that it's imperative to dig for levity in tragedy and for the seriousness, the truth, in comedy. Zelenskyy clearly understood this tenet when he created *Servant of the People*, which gained vast popularity. Zelenskyy's production company, Kvartal 95, set out in the show to mock Ukraine's political elite and to highlight the country's corruption. Sure, it might have been simplified or exaggerated for laughs, like most productions. But its basis was Truth, with a capital T.

"The best way to make sure Ukrainians don't come to accept the current state of affairs as normal is to put these [political] absurdities in a new format," Zelenskyy had said.

And then, as one of the show's writers revealed, "It's not a story about how things are, but how they should be. That's why people are watching it." And that's why people voted for its star creator.

In hindsight, we now see how Zelenskyy's fate practically paved itself. His love of performance and of truth thrived in a country that had been maimed by years of a corrupt Soviet regime, followed by puppet leaders and oligarchs looking out for their own interests. His political humor was rooted in reality, and his popularity opened doors to the next logical step: his leadership of a nation that needed it.

Now, let us not put on rose (or yellow and blue) colored glasses and pretend that Zelenskyy has been a perfect leader. That's not it at all—nor is that doable, especially in a country recovering from decades of subjugation. What he was—in stark contrast to what had come before him—is honest. He was honest, for instance, in his goal to find a diplomatic peace with Russia, to solve the years-long conflict in Donbas with as little bloodshed as possible. He was the opposite of hawkish, and his stance differed from that of other Ukrainians. Putin's immovable imperialistic aims, however, made Ze's desire for peace irrelevant. Yet even as he was dealing with the undesirable actuality, he remained open with his people.

Nightly, Ze would lay out the problems Ukraine was facing, the tragic losses it incurred, and he would detail what he was doing to help combat that—how he was recruiting help from the rest of the free world, his government's plans for rebuilding what's been lost, his hope for returning peace to Ukraine. He has been more forthcoming and emotionally honest than, perhaps, any leader we have ever seen. (I mean, he addressed his citizens every. Single. Night. Whatever state he was in.) He constantly managed to reveal the challenges, the atrocities, and his hope in one breath. And he did so continuously, day after day.

"Our weapon is our truth," he said at the start of the war, "and our truth lies in the fact that this is our land, this is our country, our children, and we are going to defend all of that. . . . Glory to Ukraine!"

Wiggle Room

Zelenskyy's truthfulness was in stark contrast to the propaganda machine fueled by Putin in Russia—a machine that had been operating for eons. The bulk of people who grew up under Soviet rule developed a distrust of government, taking everything they were told with a grain of salt, if that. And let's not kid ourselves, even government in America has not honored the trust of its people, not by a long shot. This same situation has shown up all over the world, in fact, no matter how advanced the country—officials sacrificing truth for power, covering up what doesn't serve them personally, and creating false narratives so convincingly that they themselves begin to believe them. That is why Zelenskyy's candor, bravery, and openness have been such a breath of fresh air.

"I want to do something to change the mistrust toward politicians," he'd said when running for president.

What we understand, in marveling at Zelenskyy's moral clarity, is that truth is not as complicated as we think (even if it's ugly). It is far simpler, for instance, than the convoluted lies told by Putin and his cronies, and simpler than even the confusion, the muddled story lines, constantly unfolding here in our own America. Of course, there is far more goodness, far more freedom in our system than in autocracies like that of Russia. But still—how democratic is a less than honest government? How can we call it a democracy if realities are covered up and twisted left and right?

There can be no true democracy without honesty—the presentation of what is, to the people you represent or lead, the good and the not so good alike. The only place where truth has wiggle room, in fact, *is* in its presentation—which is probably why our star presenter is so good at his job.

Reality can be shaped by hope or it can be shaped by cynicism. Zelenskyy presents it with hope.

Still, some truth is so harsh, it can't be delivered softly. And the most beautiful, honest plans can fall into ruins as quickly as they're concocted. Honesty, though, remains imperative for any egalitarian structure simply because people cannot make choices about that which they do not know.

Perhaps that is what we're so afraid of when we evade the truth in our relationships and personal lives as well: relinquishing control and letting others choose what to do with truth.

Democracies Everywhere

Here is the thing about lying—you may think you're doing it because it's easier or better or helps you save face in a situation. And I'm sure many politicians convince themselves they're doing what's best for their constituents, or simply what's necessary to stay in control. There are myriad reasons to lie, but only one to tell the truth: it is the right thing to do. That's what's at the core of Zelenskyy's truth-telling and raw honesty that we've found so refreshing—dignity.

Truth equals dignity.

Whether you're leading a company, navigating a relationship, or steering a family, go with truth. Speaking of which, Zelenskyy's got some domestic tips too. He joked that his family is even more of an open democracy than his country when he was asked whether he tells his kids—then a seventeen-year-old daughter and a nearly nine-year-old son—the full truth of Ukraine's dire situation in the war.

"I answer all of their questions openly," he told *60 Minutes Australia*. "I don't keep secrets from them. They clearly know what we are fighting for," he said, "and they clearly know that we will be victorious."

Zelenskyy's brand of optimistic honesty is the goal, I believe. There is always a way to be truthful, including with our little ones. Sometimes we fail at this, we take the easy way out, we lie, but using Ze as an example, can we instead look for ways to be honest, even if some sugarcoating is needed?

After all, one man's sugarcoating is another man's faith. Perhaps where candor meets hope is the sweet spot.

You too can find a way of truth-telling you're comfortable with and use it in all of life's facets—from family to work life. Do not fear the relinquishing of reins that honesty requires.

Give people the truth and let them choose/process/react for themselves. Your dignity is worth it.

7

Children as Guideposts

"I really do not want my pictures in your offices, for the president is not an icon, an idol, or a portrait," *Zelenskyy said in his 2019 inaugural address, speaking to the Verkhovna Rada.* "Hang your kids' photos instead, and look at them each time you are making a decision."

What do you think of when you think of Volodymyr Zelenskyy?

Hero, right? No matter how many times he tells us he isn't one. And wartime leader, icon, superstar.

Yet what we often forget in watching him these days, strong and steadfast in his army tees, is that he is also just a person—as he himself tries to remind us again and again. His wife, Olena, even called him sentimental, saying there are often tears in his eyes when they watch romantic films together. So . . . he's a person who cries when watching mushy movies with his wife.

Yes, Volodymyr Zelenskyy is just a person—someone's son, someone's father, someone's husband—and his family is everything to him, no less so than it is for you and for me.

"This is my *family*," he said in an early wartime interview, as if there's nothing more sacred than the very concept, "and I believe that that's my weak spot."

Our broods *are* our weak spots, aren't they? Our children, our Achilles' heel, whatever our nationality or set of beliefs—because they're our hearts, our souls, walking, talking, living outside of us and our control, outside of our ability to protect them forevermore. Can you imagine then the extent of that feeling, that vulnerability, when you're target number one for your enemies, and your family is target number two?

That was Ze's reality. It is from this space that he had to lead a nation.

At the same time—like all parents to all kids, whatever the parents' rank might be out in the world—to his children, Zelenskyy was and is, simply Dad.

Ukraine's First Lady—who herself was a pillar of unfaltering support during her country's crisis—said in an interview with the *Today* show that Ze is a "very soft and kind father; he cannot say no to his children." In another interview, she shared that her and Volodymyr's then nine-year-old son has become a military expert, giving his father advice: what ammunition their nation needs, which countries are doing a good job of supporting them, which are not.

And when talking to CNN's Jake Tapper, the Ukrainian president was kidding/not kidding about his first child—his teenager: "Without knocking [on] the door, I cannot speak with my daughter," he said. When Tapper told him he too had a teenage girl, Zelenskyy laughed. "You understand me. . . . Fourteen-year-old girl? . . . We understand."

Listening to these snidbits of family life, looking at photographs of Zelenskyy, face painted at some kids' event, laughing with his son and daughter, we're able to get a glimpse of a role that's been less in the forefront during the war but one that has actually shaped the Ukrainian president's very being: being a dad. On Father's Day, 2022, Zelenskyy posted, "Being a father is a great responsibility and a great happiness. . . . It is strength, wisdom, motivation to go forward and not to give up."

His family, his children, *are* his motivation.

As he's told interviewers during the war, he always thinks about how his children will perceive what he is doing, as well as his decisions, and he wants them to be proud of him and of their country. "[My children] are proud of Ukraine, very proud," Zelenskyy told CNN, saying, "They entertain a sincere hope in our victory." He added that kids can believe in victory without considering the cost. "They simply believe that the good shall prevail."

In letting his own kids be his guiding star, Zelenskyy is able to tap into the purity that shines so brightly within our youngest humans—the simple, beautiful belief that good will prevail—and he has long asked his fellow politicians to do the same: to make that belief their goal. In his inaugural address he urged the Verkhovna Rada (the Ukrainian parliament) to start thinking about the next generation instead of the next election when governing their country—or to free their seats for those who will. "I really do not want my pictures in your offices," he said, "for the president is not an icon, an idol or a portrait. . . . Hang your kids' photos instead, and look at them each time you are making a decision."

Parenting the World

Time and time again, when speaking to the Verkhovna Rada, Ze has brought the focus on the nation's children—the next generation—who will inherit Ukraine, as well as the planet (he also stressed the importance of reducing the pace of climate change for future generations, seeking to align Ukraine's policy with the European Green Deal). In a way, by becoming his nation's president, he became a father not just to his son and daughter, but to all the children of Ukraine—and he's felt that responsibility keenly.

"I look at this, first of all, as a father," he told CNN regarding the tragic deaths of Ukrainian children in the war. "It hurts so, so much. . . . We live for our children," he added. And on International Children's Day he posted, "We will defend every Ukrainian child."

Alas, like all parents, he has had to deal with the lack of control that parenthood involves—especially in his proxy parenthood of his nation's boys and girls. There was only so much he could do to ensure their safety, which became unensurable during the war; in addition to casualties, the president revealed in June 2022 that Russia had deported thousands upon thousands of children from Ukraine, planning to make the deportees forget about their homeland.

Still, day after day, Zelenskyy did his job, leading and praising his hardworking defenders and keeping Ukraine and its youngsters at the forefront of the rest of the world's psyche. In a passionate discussion with Ukrainian child refugees, he said, "We will do everything we can to bring you all back. Bring all of you back as children, not adults, bring you back soon. It is very important for us that *you* build our country and our future because you are our beautiful future for which we are all fighting today."

In watching his expanded version air of fatherhood, we are reminded of our collective responsibility to the children in each of our nations, our communities, our families. Many of us, upon becoming parents, began to feel this responsibility acutely, and it has only grown. We love our kids so much, we ache for them and work for them and dream and plan and hope for them. But on a deeper level, I think we also understand that all kids are our kids. That's why our hearts break here in America when yet another school shooting takes place, and when war rips youngsters away from their homes and families across the world . . . when kids go hungry, when they're bullied or hurt or worse.

What do we do with all this responsibility, though? How do we not collapse under the weight of it?

Here too, Zelenskyy's words give us guidance. As he

posted in a wartime video, "For our next generations to have a future, our generation has no right to give up."

It is that simple, then. We *must* keep going, keep working on bettering this complex world of ours, and on improving unacceptable circumstances—step-by-step, one right decision at a time. As Ze said, giving up is not an option.

Also, "Hang your kids' photos instead, and look at them each time you are making a decision," he'd told his parliament, which is just as clear and actionable a suggestion for us, mere citizens. It can guide us in voting, in where we place our money, in the causes and companies we support, as well as in our personal decisions.

When we put our innocent children—and the world's innocent children—at the forefront of our minds, we are that much more likely to channel our Inner Zelenskyy, our moral clarity. Which, in fact, is how shifts happen—one moral decision, one awake individual at a time.

Childish Wisdom

In the spring of 2022, a volunteer working at a support center with children from Mariupol shared on Facebook her profound experience. She wrote about how she tried to engage two brothers in conversation by asking them about home. The older boy said sadly, "The city is gone," for it had been decimated, destroyed, leveled. Yet the younger brother replied, "in a frank and kind voice," as the volunteer put it, "But you are always welcome to visit it. The sea is still there."

From the mouths of babes, as they say, the little boy's words were then shared even more widely by President Zelenskyy: "The city is gone but the sea is still there."

And so it was. Because the sweet wisdom of children is breathtaking. It's guileless and profound. And it's true.

As Zelenskyy explained, the way kids simply believe that good will prevail, without any qualifiers. . . . We adults can use some of their untainted belief, can't we?

For children see things more lucidly than we do at times. Sure, their views may be simplistic, but ours have become overly complicated. Which is why we should listen to them a bit more keenly when dealing with the "big stuff." After all, it is they who will inherit our world.

Four months into the war Zelenskyy echoed this clarity when he explained that while life has changed greatly for Ukrainians in the war, while the path has changed, "the goal remained the same."

"We are fighting for the future of our children and grandchildren," he said, "for their life and opportunity to build a new Ukraine."

More Listening

In his inaugural address, Ze recalled how his then six-year-old son said, "Dad, they say on TV that Zelenskyy is the president. . . . So it means that I am the president too?!" The elder president laughed at his son's quip but then realized that, in fact, he was right. "Because each of us *is* the president," he said, "not just the 73 percent who voted for me, but all 100 percent of Ukrainians. . . . Each of us has just put his hand on the Constitution and swore allegiance to Ukraine."

I don't think even Zelenskyy knew how prophetic his 2019 words would be—for the people's collective allegiance to Ukraine is what kept it from dissolving into Russia when the latter attacked. Without this allegiance, without the belief in goodness that kids carry so beautifully and lightly, and without a leader who looks to youth for motivation, a free Ukraine would have ceased to exist.

So from the mouths of babes, Ukrainians were reminded, as soon as Zelenskyy was elected, that each of them was responsible for the country's future.

And across the world we, too, can become better listeners to the children in our lives and to their inherent wisdom. Despite the well-worn hierarchy where we are their wards, teachers, and leaders, we must remember to let them take the reins from time to time, as well as to heed what they are trying to tell us.

The city may be gone but the sea is still there, as a little boy once said.

Quel Legacy

In America, where politics has become a jumbled web of complexity and infuriation, I love hearing my kids' takes on how things should be. "I think the rule should be that only someone who has kids can become president," my then seven-year-old said, adding, "or it could be someone who is a teacher . . . someone who knows how to take care of kids."

Like Zelenskyy, I laughed and then realized how right she was. "Someone who knows how to take care of kids" would surely make a great qualifying factor for the chance to lead a nation, though maybe we could change the wording a tad. *Someone who actually cares about kids*—someone who sees them as a guidepost, like Zelenskyy does—only that kind of person should get the opportunity to run for government. Certainly then the gun violence problem in our country could be solved—or at least could begin to be solved? And maybe other unsolvable problems would too become solvable.

As Ze said, "I do not understand our government that only shrugs and says: 'There is nothing we can do.' Not true. You can. You can take a sheet of paper and a pen and free your seats for those who think about the next generations and not about the next election!"

Same here, Ze, same here.

And, in fact, if we keep children—our children, our nation's children, the world's children—at the forefront of our minds when we have even simpler life decisions to make . . . well, we know that at least we'll be moving toward a reality where "the good shall prevail."

So let's let the children lead *us* (I mean, we don't need to tell them about it; they might get drunk on all the power—and sugar). Let's ask ourselves, *What would my child—or simply, a child—think about what I'm doing right now? How might a child approach this problem . . . like, after their tantrum?*

For us parents, the question *How will this affect my kids?* is such a potent guiding force. For companies, *How will this affect the town's, the country's, or the world's kids?* is also a vital inquiry.

Let us not leave the next generation out of the equation any longer; we just happened to be born first, is all. For even as we navigate our own paths, create our adult messes and problems, it is their legacy that we are ultimately deciding.

8

Let Freedom Echo

Russia has attacked not just us, not just our land, not just our cities; it went on a brutal offensive against our values, basic human values. It threw tanks and planes against our freedom, against our right to live freely in our own country choosing our own future. . . .

—*Zelenskyy addressing the US Congress*
several weeks into the war

Let's not mince words—the war Russia launched in Ukraine was an absolute catastrophe, and a shocking one at that.

This war was a doozy that Vladimir Putin had obviously been planning for a long, long time—though much of the world hadn't realized it. In hindsight, we can see more clearly the mindset that led him to aggression, and the mindset with which he infected a lot of his countrymen: the idea that the dissolution of the Soviet Union was the greatest tragedy of the twentieth century (his words, not mine). This imperialistic nationalism, in fact, was at the core of Russia's sense of self—a powerful country that ruled over many of its neighbors—with Putin and his cronies entertaining all sorts of ideas as to why Russia deserved to do so, and how it was the antidote to America and to the West.

But the fact is—as imperfect as America, Europe, "the West" may be—what we're based on is the most basic of human desires, which burns brightly in all of us upon birth: freedom. And freedom is just not something Russia believes in for the average citizen.

What to Do

"Our people need freedom like a monkey needs glasses," a party administrator says in the book *Secondhand Time*—an oral history by Svetlana Alexievich of the Soviet Union's final days. "No one would know what to do with it."

And maybe they wouldn't; some had never really gotten to experience it.

The reality is, though, that we humans inherently seek freedom—it is part of our DNA. And while the desire to be free can be subdued with force and over decades of repression, it's like an ember just waiting to be fanned—which is exactly what the oppressors fear. Anyone whose main goal is the control of and power over others is constantly wary of whatever may fan the embers of freedom within their subjugated population.

For Putin, the problem was that—when it came to his imperialistic aims—Ukrainians were no longer an oppressed population, and squeezing free people back into a tube of constraint proved much harder than he had realized.

As Volodymyr Zelenskyy said, "We have tasted freedom and we will not give it up," referring to Ukraine's self-determination since the fall of the USSR. And anyone who had escaped Soviet restraints knew exactly what Ze was talking about (anyone who escaped any restraints, really). When freedom is reignited within you, there's no putting it out. And it is certainly a value worth fighting for, since without it you're not fully living.

So how do you take freedom away from people who've already tasted it? Or how about those born into it, after the freedomless empire collapsed?

If you're Putin, you jail or kill your critics and you brainwash your citizens with endless propaganda, until they do not know any better—or if they do, they must suppress the yearning to be free in order to live, even if unfreely.

The reality is, Russia's war was not just an attack on Ukraine; it was an attack on freedom as a whole—including an assault on the freedom of its own people and on any people it could overcome by force. As Zelenskyy told the world a month after Putin's troops invaded, "The war of Russia is not only the war against Ukraine; its meaning is much wider. Russia started the war against freedom as it is. . . . Russia is trying to defeat the freedom of all people in

Europe, of all the people in the world. It tries to show that only crude and cruel force matters."

Well, when Ze put it like that, how could anyone *not* support him?

You either supported Ukraine or you didn't fully value freedom—he made that clear to us. And to *not* value freedom is to not value life in all its fullness . . . it is to not value possibility.

"We are defending the ability of a person to live in the modern world," Zelenskyy told *60 Minutes*. "We are defending the right to live. . . . So that Russia doesn't choose what we should do," he added, "and how I am exercising my rights. That right was given to me by God and my parents."

This right, by the way, is also one we must give to ourselves, as well as to one another. That's as good of a place to start as any.

Taste of Freedom

Soviet schools required uniforms for children, which most of us didn't mind at six or seven when we had to start wearing them. *Less to think about*, it seemed, not to mention that no one had much clothing to choose from—a second dress or pair of pants was a luxury. Plus, it was just what you did.

Everything was so orderly, so predictable with your one dress and your school uniform. You always knew what to expect in the classroom, for instance, and what was expected of you. *Sit quietly, listen, raise your hand just so and no higher.* (You had to perch with one arm on top of the other, neatly folded at your desk, and to speak, you could raise your top arm at the elbow, so it would be perfectly perpendicular to the bottom one—this and only this was the way hands were raised.)

Holy moly did American classrooms seem like carnivals to me after I left the USSR—kids talking loudly, endless running to and fro, arms waving all over the place. . . . They were so unruly, so . . . free. Like Putin, I was initially disgusted by this freedom. And I was only eight.

My point here is that freedom can seem vapid, crazy, and self-indulgent when you've never had very much. My point is, please do not hate Russian people as a whole. *Forgive them, they know not what they do,* as Jesus would say. So many of them do not know any better; so many of them probably never will.

But as our man Ze explained, once you do get to taste freedom, you are not likely to give it back—Ukrainians certainly weren't. And once you fully experience it, you're more than willing to break out of the cage of oppression and to venture forth, even if it's scary, unpredictable, dangerous. Then you can fight using the full force of the freedom within you in order to protect it. You can fight like a modern-day David—or Zelenskyy—no matter how big your Goliath. You can fight until you win or die trying, which is why as Ze said in April 2022, "Freedom must be armed better than tyranny."

Plus, lest we forget—freedom, more than anything, is an internal game. As Ze stated in a speech to Stanford University in May, "Our cities are destroyed. Our sea is still blocked. But we remain free." And "We are the free people of independent Ukraine," he declared defiantly on its Independence Day.

Inner Tyranny

Now, while a nation like Ukraine has no choice but to fight for its freedom, our personal liberty, too, can require an army of sorts to defeat its inner or generational tyranny.

For instance, what can be so exasperating for immigrant families—especially those from oppressive places like the USSR—is that they may come to a free country, but they can't always give their children the freedom they need to flourish as individuals; they can't always give it to themselves. More so, many of us humans—wherever we come from, whatever our background—live in cages of our own creation, following someone else's rules, fulfilling someone else's expectations, whether these are familial or societal or based on keeping up with those darn Joneses.

The external noise is ridiculous in this era of ours, when we're bombarded by social media, emails, the news, the experts, the advertisements. See, the foes to our freedom are not always as horrific as Putin—they come in more subtle forms too—and if we're not careful, we can end up creating our own shackles, our own inner prisons. We can end up less than free even without a clear-cut enemy disempowering us. Because "the enemy" can be far more complicated and obscure than an outside regime.

Six Degrees of Liberty

These days, America too finds itself in its own struggle for freedom. It seems as if there are internal forces flexing their power here—as opposed to an external Putin—and they are out to curb the liberties we've had for decades. And it feels dangerous . . . but not insurmountable.

When freedom starts slipping away from us—from those who've had it for so long, who've perhaps taken it for granted—the good news is, we wake up to its importance in our lives.

Like Ukraine, we, America, have been rudely awakened. We must now redefine our own freedom as well. Still, let us remember how lucky we are to be able to fight with words and with laws, instead of with tanks and bombs. The Ukrainians didn't have such a choice. Let us remember that our country is a self-correcting democracy—and it's on us to help it correct itself.

Zelenskyy's powerful speeches made us understand that what we were seeing in Ukraine was a clash of ideas—one being the modern idea of freedom and democracy and the other being the rule of crude force. In a way, we're seeing the same conflict play out here in the US. In a way, it is present everywhere on the globe.

And so as you speak up for the freedoms at stake wherever you live, wherever you find yourself—whether you vote in support of these liberties, finance them, or even don fatigues in order to protect them like so many Ukrainians have had to do—eventually you will also need to go within and do the same. Because oppression is in our bones in one way or another—sadly, it is our human history—and our bones, too, beg to be set right.

So you will need to talk to yourself about freedom.

Am I living freely? You'll need to ask your heart—and only you will know the answer. *Am I letting others live freely?*

Free Others

Remember how in speaking about his family, Zelenskyy joked that it too is a free country? He talked about the openness with which he and Olena raise their children. That is the kind of family structure I also yearn for. In fact, it seems to me the perfect blueprint for any kind of structure: a family, a company, an organization.

Those of us who were born into oppression understand the desire to let freedom reign in our homes, as well as wherever we may roam. And peace-based philosophies like that of the Tao Te Ching, too, teach about the importance of freedom, whoever you're in charge of, whoever you may lead. For there is but a delicate difference between encouragement and control, between communication and force, between assistance and constraint.

Can we talk and explain more and force less when it comes to our children? Or even "let's make a deal," as my kids often propose, rather than turning to the old "because I said so" credo?

Are we manipulating our relationships to get others to

behave the way we'd like them to? Because that too is a form of control. Have we become reliant on cajoling, intimidating, or pleading to get what we want?

These are trick questions, by the way—don't answer them; we have all used freedomless tactics from time to time. But let us take this opportunity right now to stop. Let's let go of the reins that we've tethered to others—even if only for today. Let's enjoy how good, how *free* it feels.

And as we are freeing others, like the wild horses they all are at their core, let us not forget to free ourselves.

Free Yourself

Our lives, even in the freest of nations (or especially there), are full of tough choices. We must always be vigilant to choose *for* ourselves, rather than against. And we must hold on to our self-determination in every relationship—from spouses to families to bosses, friends, clients, and so on.

Relationships, of course, require compromise. But compromise, too, is an option, not an order—a choice to nurture the bond you value . . . or not. Because being free is not about getting your way all the time; it's about not betraying yourself.

Your job in your personal life is simple then (and also complex, and also important). Be vigilant of where and to whom you commit your time and power. Be wary of all your yeses. Listen to your core, your inner voice, your spirit, and don't betray it for anyone. And if you've ended up in a state of being spent, start taking back your time, your energy, your liberties little by little.

Make sure you fight for yourself the way Zelenskyy has shown us to fight for our values. Speak up, don't let obstacles stop you. Rest, of course, but then continue on your path toward whatever it is you've chosen. Remember what Ze said: "That right was given to me by God."

It was also given to you.

As he told the audience at the Glastonbury Festival in the summer of 2022, "Prove that freedom always wins!"

9

Unstick Yourself

We will win this war, even if individual politicians are still unable to overcome the indecision they will pass on to their successors together with their offices.

—*President Zelenskyy said after discovering the horrors that were left behind by the Russian troops in Bucha.*

We have each known the feeling of being stuck at some point in our lives—of being stagnant. In fact, it is a state that's kind of representative of the world we live in, as certain realities, certain suffering, seem cyclical: violence, destruction, oppression, war. It can feel like we are but holograms of the very world we inhabit. And it is hard enough to get ourselves out of ruts, but then, *What's the point?* Isn't the world just one big rut, anyway?

Listen, I get it. Sh*t feels bleak at times, and impossible. And since governments are but collections of imperfect humans, it is no wonder that this dark line of thinking lurks behind their decisions—or indecisions—as well.

That is why it's understandable how politicians can lack conviction, lack decisiveness, even in situations where the decision seems black-and-white: support Ukraine fully, stop enabling Russia's war machine. It sounds easy enough (except for fear of nuclear war and all that, but more on fear in the next couple chapters). Yet many governments are missing whatever is necessary to "overcome the indecision," as Zelenskyy put it.

Structures of Stuckness

As individuals, we can explicably feel hopeless, stuck, and impotent in a messed-up world. And while governments are just a bunch of individuals, their job is to transcend their human frailty. But in the very moment when their decisiveness is needed most, they can become trapped, fragile humans once more, unable to change the course of history. . . . Well, luckily, not all of them.

In many instances President Zelenskyy spoke about the indecision of politicians throughout the world to *fully* support Ukraine's struggle for freedom and humanity. Ukraine needed more weapons, more aid, more sanctions against its aggressor. It was dealing with a tyrant far more powerful and well-armed. And it needed the world to stand up and say "Not okay" to the cruel actions of said tyrant. Not okay, period—no more business dealings, no more trade, no more oil, no more gas purchased from Russia.

Weapons, support, closed skies. Immediately.

Could you imagine the situation in Ukraine had the powers of the world stood up to that degree collectively and quickly?

Ze pointed out that numerous international atrocities were allowed to take place in the recent past, "from Syria to Somalia, from Afghanistan to Yemen and Libya. . . . If tyranny had ever received such a response to the war it had unleashed," he pointed out, "it would have ceased to exist . . . and the world would have changed for sure." He said then perhaps Ukraine wouldn't be facing so much tragedy today.

Zelenskyy reminded us of our collective human failure to decide, once and for all, that we cannot allow tyranny to take root *anywhere*, that the peaceful (and powerful) nations will not stand for it. And he called out the UN Security Council—whose permanent members include China and Russia—on its inability to guarantee security. He challenged it to either remove the Russian Federation—due to it being the very source of war—so that it would stop blocking decisions made about its own aggression, or to "dissolve yourselves altogether."

"Are you ready to close the United Nations?" he asked. "Do you think that the time for international law is gone?"

He made us see clearly—whether we wanted to or not—that indecision and lack of conviction keep the world stuck in a pattern of pain and in cycles of violence. Of course, the same is true on a personal level: indecision can also keep us stuck for ages in less than happy, less than healthy, even soulless situations . . . or it can simply stop us from doing what's best for ourselves, keeping us from growing, thriving, and bettering the world, one itty bitty person at a time.

Paralysis through Analysis

The idea of analysis paralysis is very real for overthinkers and "bad decision makers"—which is how I used to think of myself, unable to choose a meal or what to watch or what to wear . . . or what to study, or pursue, or do with my life. Soviet culture had little choice, Western culture had lots; it felt like whiplash to go from the former to the latter. Plus, most of us suffer from the paradox of choice at some point—the paradox that while more choices offer more opportunities, they can also submerge us in indecision, paralyzing us via our overthinking of all the different routes we can take.

Yet simply by choosing, by walking, by acting on something, on anything, we each end up walking the way—our way. And though this way may have many a wrong turn or "failure," can't we just view failures as detours in a righter-for-us direction?

And so we learn not to overthink but to move. Not to wait for perfection but to type out the words on the keyboard as they come. Not to figure out the ideal solution, but to try any solution and run with it, and then course-correct as needed.

*　　*　　*

For organizations, for groups of people, for governments, paralysis through analysis is often as big a problem as for us overthinkers. When cohorts try to wade through all the scenarios, they find even more scenarios to wade through. When they consider all the risks and fears, there are that many more risks and fears to consider. And when they attempt to come up with a perfect solution—especially a "safe" solution—they get stuck. And in that stuckness nothing happens, or nothing good at least. And we patch things up and continue on, but only until the next big problem rears its head—the next recession, the next shooting, the next war—and then we start the process all over again.

But what Zelenskyy has reminded us is that some scenarios are so clear—aggressor versus peace-lover, for instance, or imperialist versus nation minding its own business—that there's no need to waste time, to overanalyze, to incur the dreaded analysis paralysis. The key is to act decisively and swiftly, to kick the tyrant's butt, to stare the bully in the face and to do the right thing.

That kind of moral clarity takes guts, it takes all of our Inner Zelenskyys. And Ukraine needs it, the world needs it. We need it.

Jolts of Unstickiness

Anxiety is relieved through action—whether it's action chosen by you or one that is thrust upon you by an outside force. Take the situation in Ukraine, for one. The nation had been asking America and the rest of Europe for help with modern missile defense even before a full-scale war began. After Russia did invade on February 24 (an example of an outside force acting upon the whole world, really), help came in bits and trickles. Zelenskyy said as much, calling out the indecision of nations that couldn't agree to stop trade with Russia, to stop doing business with its banks, to stop buying its oil. But with each instance of extreme terror, the world moved toward greater support for his nation, toward providing better weapons and defense. And each time this happened, many of us could not help but think, *Why just now? Why not sooner?* Why must forces of evil push us into action—can't we decide on that action for ourselves, before the terrible price of lives and limbs?

Like thousands of people across the world, I was in a mall with my children shortly after their school year ended in 2022. It happened to be the same day that Russian missiles hit a mall in Kremenchuk, in central Ukraine, killing dozens and injuring many more. This was far from the first or the last act of terror unleashed on civilians by Putin's army. And it became impossible to ignore the parallels of our two worlds. We all went to the mall for recreation, for a touch of normalcy, for an hour of fun or shopping or socializing.

How is it that only some of us got to enjoy such an innocent activity without the threat of a fiery demise?

America understood the tragedy—and the terror that still loomed large; Europe understood it, with the G7 leaders immediately calling the attack a war crime. But couldn't they have understood it a little sooner? After all, Russia had already fired missiles upon a theater, a maternity hospital, upon apartment buildings, and upon folks waiting in line for bread. Russia had already blocked tons of wheat exports from Ukraine that were so badly needed in other parts of the world. Russia had already destroyed so much, not the least of which was peace, which Europe had come to rely on.

And yet the powers of the world couldn't or didn't move past their indecision, past their stuckness, until terrible things occurred—in bits and trickles. With each terrible thing came a jolt forward in their support of Ukraine's fight against autocracy, against terrorism.

So the question beckons, *Is there a better way to get unstuck?*

The Good and the Bad

Let's tackle the bad news first, to get it out of the way. The bad is this: there's no simple answer to our geopolitical problems. That is fact. At least not in our current complex, precarious geopolitical system. It's easy in hindsight to say the powers that be didn't act enough—not early enough and not with enough conviction—to stop Russian aggression, violence, terror in Ukraine. Many of us felt this from the onset; no one more so than Ze, of course.

However, from the point of view of other leaders responsible for entire countries—well, the risk of starting a larger war, a world war, with a nuclear power like Russia, was ridiculously huge. Now, we can easily guess how Zelenskyy feels about acting from a place of fear (more on that coming up), but we must admit that as regular citizens, we don't know what we don't know. And many of us would never want to be in a decision-making position of that level: How much can we help defend our peaceful friends before poking the nuclear bear one poke too hard?

The good news, though, is that indecision on a personal level does *not* have nuclear consequences. Yes, there are always consequences, but moving past our individual stuckness is a less frightful process—or at least it can be.

Zelenskyy had clearly communicated to us how important it is to get unstuck, to overcome indecision in the world. What we can do right now is to implement this advice on a personal and micro level. And once again, Ze has left us clues as to how.

Ze's Clues

The key to unsticking ourselves is to connect to our core, to our deepest beliefs. Many of us have not done that in a long while—so let's ask ourselves, *What* are *my core values, beliefs, guideposts for life?* It's a helpful sort of internal inquiry.

And once we've got that basis in place, acting in accordance with it is all that's needed. It's our Inner Zelenskyy, in other words, who says things like, "I need ammunition, not a ride" in a time of crisis. It's the clarity that lets us act and move forward, including through fear. It allows us to try things that may or may not work out, but at least we become willing to try them.

That is how we learn to imagine ourselves into being—which happens to be what masters like Zelenskyy have known all along.

Think about Ze as a young man falling in love with performance after the crumbling of the Soviet Union, finding himself through both gaudy and insightful humor, pretending to be, then becoming, the man to change Ukraine for the better. Wasn't his imagination his first step in formation?

Zelenskyy was especially drawn to improv and sketch comedy, co-creating a troupe and participating in comedy competitions which paved his way in the entertainment business. And as many an artist knows, there is a freedom from fear and self-consciousness that eventually arises when you're performing for laughs, performing live and in the moment. It can be frightful and thrilling, both, but the idea behind improv is to be as present as possible to catch the laugh, catch the funny as it takes place—line by line, from one person's imagination to the next. There is no room for paralysis through analysis when you are in the present moment—free from past doubts and future anxiety—and presence, too, is a key to getting unstuck.

Finally, as you learn to embody—to imagine, to pretend, to conjure, and to bring yourself back to the now, saying

F-off to the past, to your insecurities, and to the fear of failure—when you do all that, there is but one move left: to do. You take one little step and then another and another, and before you know it you've walked yourself out of your rut. You may not know where the bleep you are or where on this green earth you are going, but at least you're out of the stuckness.

So 1) imagine your unstuck self and embody him or her—play pretend, 2) practice presence, so there's no room for talking yourself out of it via fear or insecurity—the dreaded paralysis, and 3) take a step forward, even if it's a little one, and just keep steppin'.

You can use this method—inspired by our one and only Ze—in business, in relationships, in career and life questions big and small, and you too will "win this war," even if your war is only with yourself.

10

From Fear to Love

I need ammunition, not a ride.

—*Zelenskyy's response to America's offer to evacuate
him from Kyiv at the start of the war*

According to the 1976 spiritual work *A Course in Miracles*—
which has been dubbed the New Age Bible *and* called sa-
tanic, depending on whom you ask—there are but two
emotions that we can experience in this life: love and fear.
Those are the two categories that all our internal states can
be boiled down to, and then we're either dealing with the
energy of love or with the energy of fear.

I find this perspective so useful because I picture it as a
continuum: fear on one end, love on the other—with lots of

nuances in between—and any conundrum we look at can then be approached from one or the other.

When we stop to consider our choices as such, the choice often makes itself.

Fearlessness

Most of us wouldn't consciously choose fear as our motivator, right? Certainly not Volodymyr Zelenskyy, who so famously said *No* when America offered to extricate him from Ukraine once Russia invaded.

It was an understandable offer: Zelenskyy was Russia's target number one—he had said so himself, and his security team later thwarted multiple assassination attempts. Still, those close to the president said it wasn't even a question for him as to whether to stay or not. Fear did not factor in because he so naturally walks the way of love.

His country was being attacked. He was the rightfully elected president of said country. He and his people wanted freedom and self-determination. Rooted in the love he felt for his nation, his post, the people he represented, he said, "The fight is here; I need ammunition, not a ride."

It was his immediate resolve that shaped the fate of history. His cabinet followed his lead; officials who had left returned. Russia's plans to swiftly take over were thwarted by the energy of love.

Then, weeks into the war, Zelenskyy addressed the mothers of the thousands of Russian soldiers who had become stranded in Ukraine in the fight they neither chose, nor even understood, in the case of many (some were initially told they were being sent to do military exercises). "We do not [need] Russian soldiers. We didn't want this war," Zelenskyy said to the Russian mothers. "We only want peace. And we want you to love your children more than you fear your authorities."

We only want peace. And we want you to love your children more than you fear your authorities.

The beauty of his statement still sends shivers down my own motherly spine.

Ze was urging these mamas—the frightened Russian citizens, trained to bend to their authoritarian leaders over years of generational trauma—he was urging them all to choose love over fear.

Origins of Fear

Fear happens to be a swampy sucker—the longer you allow it to take control, the harder it is to break out of. It's not impossible, of course, just . . . swampy.

The Russian people—whom Zelenskyy would frequently address in his early wartime videos, switching from a Ukrainian to a Russian dialect—had been living in this swamp for eons. They paid homage to fear and listened to it as they were told. I knew this viscerally. This Soviet-era fear-domination was one I was born into myself. It's such a big part of my having been a good Soviet child, a people-pleasing girl, a studious young woman. The child who proudly wore a little red star with Lenin's face on it because

I believed that my government, brought into being by this Lenin, was *the* government. My authority figures were *the* authority figures.

This fear, this adherence, had been programmed into the Russian psyche for so long that it was not an easy habit to break—not for me, the Soviet child growing up in America, and certainly not for scared Russian citizens who'd been scared in perpetuity.

I am one of the lucky ones. My parents didn't buy into the fear. The love in their hearts had won even before my birth. My dad, a lover of the banned Beatles and of bell-bottoms and of his guitar, had joined my mom in her dream of freedom—my mom who had been born to parents sent to languish in Siberia by Stalin's administration of fear. And yet her father would secretly listen to Voice of America on the radio, perhaps envisioning a future that my own children would get to live out.

My dad, born in Ukraine, his father like Zelenskyy's grandfather having been a World War II hero—a battalion commander of the Second Ukrainian Front, he'd been thrice injured—his family, like Zelenskyy's family, having survived the Holocaust. . . . Well, what can I say? We come from war-torn people; like Ze's lineage, mine are survivors. And what survivors know how to do is put one scared foot in front of the other—for fear is not the absence of love, but just a distance we need to cross.

My parents, brother, and I—along with Babushka and my uncle's family—left the Soviet Union after I finished second grade. I got to grow up in this wonderful, ridiculous-in-its-own-way country. Now I live with my American husband

and daughters in that idyllic American town where my problems range from suburban squabbles to the occasional coyote-spotting. Still, my heart sometimes pounds against my chest with the adrenaline of my early displacement and confusion—the programming to obey, the things I thought I was supposed to be, the lackluster way in which I was greeted here by peers.

And yet this same early pain that pushed me to the brink with teenage eating disorders, with grown-up anxiety and depression—it forced me to trade in my fright; it forced me on my knees, from which only love made sense. This fright that was handed to me at birth or soon thereafter—the anxiety of my Holocaust-surviving babushka, my Siberia-born mama, and the DNA of the rest of my ancestors who ran for their lives, as well as of those who'd perished. I traded in their fear because, after all, America does offer choice. It does offer freedom, even if imperfect—the very choice, the very freedom that Ukrainian people had too claimed as their own.

It was the love within me, though sometimes overshadowed, that eventually led me to seek spiritual answers and soulful healing. It led me on a path to ancient philosophy and to my own intuitive power, until reaching for love became second nature. Choosing from love, returning to love.

"Empires are built through economics, not through intimidation," Zelenskyy told Russian journalists in March 2022, intimating that Putin's use of fear cannot make Russia successful—rather it does the opposite. Internal success, individual success also cannot be created in fear. But to combat it, we need to go to its origin.

Programming

So let's talk fear now—this feeling that grips us, striking us immobile, or worse yet, has us lash out or barrel forward over others, or upends our lives as we do everything in our power to avoid "bad" circumstances. This terror—this freeze, fight, or flight—has been programmed in us since the big bang, practically.

We started out here on this earth as simply animals, right? And for animals, fear is a protective agent. I used to watch my scaredy-cat of a cat and laugh, his instincts making him hide under the couch the second the doorbell rang. We too do that—we too hide, and it is totally fine—I write this from my bed, for instance, under the covers, which make me feel safer in a world at war. Mistakes are made, though, when major life and geopolitical decisions arise from a scared place. It's as if that's the only way we know how to operate collectively, not realizing that the fear is at least as damaging as whatever caused it, whatever it's trying to avoid.

Covid, for example, was doubly awful—once for the havoc the disease wreaked, and again because of the pandemic of anxiety it created.

And then Vladimir Putin, steeped in fear, invaded Ukraine, citing all sorts of bullshit reasons, like the laughable goal to liberate Ukraine from Nazis. In reality, whatever his actual motive was, fear was behind it: fear of the West, of losing power, of freedom seeping in and usurping his sphere of influence. Fear that cost thousands of lives—the lives of Ukrainian civilians and of Russian soldiers, of animals and of trees and cities wiped off the face of the earth. And it is fright that kept the Russian population compliant—traumatized for ages by tyrants who gave them so much to be afraid of. (Joseph Stalin, who ruled the Soviet Union for a quarter century, killed millions upon millions of his own people, and sent millions more to camps in Siberia, for instance.)

And yet there are always those who don't give in to fear— the Russian citizens who protested Putin's war, even as they were beaten and jailed. The entire nation of Ukraine, which stood up to defend its freedom. Volodymyr Zelenskyy, in all his humanity, who met tragedy with dignity.

And so it was.

Dissolving Fear

If I am honest with you, I hear the call of fear quite frequently these days—despite all of my spiritual knowledge. But the good part is, *because* of this knowledge, because of years of internal work, I've developed the awareness to see it for what it is, to recognize it. Because feeling afraid isn't the problem—it's simply our programming—but it is the bending to that feeling that breaks us. When we are asleep, we tend to give in to this programming without questioning it. When we evolve to see it more clearly, we can do better.

In my own small way, I bare my soul with my work, even though it's scary. I go out and tell the truth the way I experience it. And then I go back to my bed. Sometimes I have what's known as a vulnerability hangover, because fear takes on a thousand faces: *Oh no, I've been too honest, everyone saw me, I've been exposed, I need to hide*. And then I want to stay in my bed forever. And truly, those days I need to dig for the love just to get out of said bed. Because I am not as natural a spiritual leader as Zelenskyy—or at least I don't think of myself as such (I doubt Zelenskyy does either, for that matter). But I am a good interpreter. And as a spiritual interpreter, I understand the importance of the lessons he's shown the world.

Do what's right, he was telling us with his actions, *because when you act out of love, fear disappears*.

The fear disappears in the doing—no need to wait for it to pass. It changes form as you go along. Perhaps it lingers as discomfort, but it doesn't have to be a block that stops you.

Zelenskyy didn't leave; he stayed. He led his people through a war, even when the leading simply meant being there, sticking it out, doing his best.

I got out of bed.

How about you?

Down the Rabbit Hole

While love is an energy of indomitable strength, fear is not. Of course, it wins sometimes too—this is not paradise, after all. Not yet, anyway. But I see fear as simply the gray clouds that block love's sun. And it presents itself in a myriad of forms that damage our lives and our world: greed, righteousness, hatred. At its peak, as fear produces ever more fear, it manifests as war.

Love is there all along, though, even when we can't feel it due to the pollution that fright has created. And so we think it's missing, but it is not—it's overshadowed. "Even Hitler loved dogs," as they say. As does Putin, by the way.

Now let us not dissect the fraught, downward path of sick-in-the-head autocrats who've caused needless bloodshed and suffering. But I will say that when you immerse yourself in the world's spiritual teachings long enough, you begin to understand that *even* those autocrats began with love. Have you ever seen a baby who hasn't?

"But what does all this love, fear, and geopolitics talk have to do with me?" you may ask.

Well, I'll tell you.

One of my great *Aha!* moments was the understanding that "as within so without," that the struggles we face within us are often the struggles we see play out on the world stage, and vice versa. Our internal world corresponds to the external one, because we live in the Universe and the Universe lives within us. And often, major world catastrophes are representative of what we do to one another and to ourselves on an individual level.

The love-versus-fear phenomenon is one that's clear as can be in the lives of everyday people. It presents itself time and time again, with every roadblock, with every big decision.

When, for example, we deal with relationship problems, be it infidelity or mistreatment or even boredom, *Should I stay or should I go?* is the question we ask ourselves—and anyone who will listen, who will go down the rabbit hole with us. And it's an instance that most of us have found

ourselves in at one time or another—or at least have con-
templated. In my case, I only fully understood the love/fear
dynamic of this circumstance once I found myself in a steady
(rather than perfect) marriage I can count on. Because life
lessons tend to show up in many different iterations until we
finally grasp them, and even afterward we may be tested, for
guarantees are few and far between.

But this hint is forever useful: if you end up in a situation where you're not sure whether to stay or go, the decision becomes easier to make when you consider love and
fear.

If you stay, are you doing this out of love—love of family, love of the other person, love for your relationship and
the willingness to work on it? Or are you staying because
you're afraid of difficult changes, of being alone, of disrupt-
ing the status quo?

Are you leaving because you're moving toward love
and leaving the fear behind? Or are you departing because
you're scared of growth, of real intimacy, or of the work
that staying takes?

Pause and think. Do so for any crossroads in which you
find yourself, no matter how small or significant. Ask yourself, *Am I making this decision from a place of love or from
a place of fear?*

Or, simply, *What would the man in the green army tee do?*

11

Decide with Courage

"Courage must be a criterion for evaluating decisions,"
Zelenskyy said in March 2022, in a video calling for
harsher sanctions against Russia upon uncovering the
atrocities in Bucha. "We will spread our courage."

The sixth Ukrainian president, Volodymyr Oleksandrovych
Zelenskyy, is brave.

Pretty much everybody on earth knows this by now.
And President Zelenskyy is loved for his courage; he is venerated for it. So it is tempting for us to then turn him into
a superhuman figure—going down in history as a larger-
than-life symbol the rest of us can but ogle at and admire.

That is not the point of this book, though (as you already

know). And Zelenskyy is not actually superhuman either. He is simply super*clear* on doing the next right thing.

We can't help but notice Ze's heroic qualities and actions, because that is what caught the world's attention in the first place—and it's what's kept our attention. But he's been quietly leaning upon courage, bravery, and faith to lead his way long before all of our eyes were upon him.

Ze's former press secretary Iuliia Mendel told interviewers that even prior to Russia's full-scale invasion, the Ukrainian president put the needs of his country ahead of his own safety. He'd fight with his security personnel, for instance, in order to go to the front lines of the conflict in Donbas; he would insist on showing support to his soldiers despite the danger, despite the personal risk involved. Mendel said, "Zelenskyy always felt that his leadership is much more important than [the] instinct of self-preservation."

Simple, right? If risking your life can ever be simple. He *chose* to supersede the human instinct of self-preservation. He was courageous, but not for the sake of being courageous. It's just that he had bigger *kotleti* to fry.

Ukrainian Brand

Zelenskyy armed himself with his own valor during the war and led Ukrainians to do the same. In the wartime videos, in his ongoing speeches and interviews, we could see it shining in his eyes, in his handshake, in his proud posture. He owned the quality; he was one with it. And he knew of its importance.

Because humans inherently understand courage is to be admired, we respect it pretty much as soon as we witness it—in those around us, as well as in ourselves. That's why Zelenskyy never missed an opportunity to highlight his people's courageous spirit in the face of war—so that the rest of the world would be aware of it as well and would support it. He praised Ukrainians every chance he got and encouraged them to be proud of themselves and of their uncrushable valor.

"In fact, this is our brand," he told them in a nightly address. "This is what it means to be us, to be Ukrainians—to be brave."

No one would argue about the bravery of a nation that was greatly underequipped and greatly lacking in manpower, yet stood up to its oppressor like nobody's business. And Zelenskyy's gutsiness—his initial move to *not* give in to fear but to stay and to lead his country, even as Russia was aiming to assassinate him—shaped history. Without it, Russia would have swiftly won as planned—as military analysts around the globe had expected.

Ze, who took his leadership more seriously than anything else, knew that only in courage lay the possibility of a better future for Ukraine. And the bulk of Ukrainians got this as well, finding the courage to do what needed to be done: men who stayed back and learned to use weapons to guard their country, women who sought a way to protect their children, ordinary citizens who cooked and organized and helped others in need.

From the earliest days of the invasion, Ukrainians showed that they weren't afraid of Putin and his forces. Remember the Ukrainian border guards at Snake Island—a Ukrainian island in the Black Sea? The Russian flagship *Moskva* began its assault on the island on day one of the war.

"This is a military warship," *Moskva* announced. "This is a Russian military warship. I suggest you lay down your weapons and surrender. . . . Otherwise, you will be bombed." To which the Ukrainian border guards replied, in arguably the coolest Slavic phrase ever uttered: *"Ruskyi voyeniy karabil, idi na huy."* ("Russian military warship, go f**k yourself.")

It made for an awesome meme/poster/stamp—like the Ukrainians created soon after. But also, it is the attitude with which one can treat all forms of fear—a bold F U—the better to defeat it with.

PS: Ukrainian forces pushed Russian troops out of Snake Island in June 2022. This small but strategic Black Sea outpost was vital for easing the passage of Ukraine's grain to other countries. . . . It was a big win. And as for the Russian warship *Moskva*? It was sunk by Ukrainian missiles a month and a half after it launched its assault.

Like fear itself when you stand up to it over and over again, the Russian military warship F'ed off—which is what it had been told to do in the first place.

Hey Fear, Go F**k Yourself

Zelenskyy kept urging the rest of the world to be as unafraid of Putin and Russia as the border guards at Snake Island were. Or to overcome the fear and to make big decisions from a place of courage. "This is not a movie, this is real life," he said in a *60 Minutes* interview. "Stop fearing the Russian Federation. We've shown we are not afraid."

Ze knew that only in finding the courage to stand up to Putin could the tyrant be stopped. Again, a nuclear threat is no small deal, but as history showed us and as Zelenskyy reminded us, giving in to fear, i.e., appeasement, only causes more disaster. And so the bulk of Ukrainians adapted that same look and stance of valor we saw in Zelenskyy and in those Snake Island border guards—a united stance that the rest of the world could not look away from.

"Who else had the courage to tell the world that hypocrisy is a bad weapon?" Zelenskyy praised his citizens. "Who else had the courage to persuade the largest global companies to forget about accounting and recall morality?"

Support may have not come all at once, but it came—in the form of aid, yes, but also in the form of dignitaries showing up in Kyiv. Politicians and stars alike came to shake hands and talk help with Ze, from Ben Stiller to Sean Penn, Richard Branson, Liev Schreiber, and Nancy Pelosi, to name a few. Sean Penn even gifted Ze one of his Oscars. "It's just a symbolic silly thing," he said, "but if I know this is here then I'll feel better."

And U2's Bono and the Edge put on a surprise concert in a Kyiv subway station. For forty minutes they played to a small crowd that gathered underground, joined by Ukrainian musicians-turned-soldiers. There were no rehearsals, no hoopla—just a simple, brave offering. "President Zelenskyy invited us to perform in Kyiv as a show of solidarity with the Ukrainian people and so that's what we've come to do," they said.

"This is also about courage," Zelenskyy proclaimed when embassies began returning to the Ukrainian capital.

He was teaching the world to lean on courage—not instead of fear but in spite of it—to choose bravery and to act on it. Fear disappears in the doing, remember? We need not wait for it to disperse.

As global citizens, we can choose the way of courage by standing up for what we believe in, even to those who disagree with us—there's plenty of need for that nationally, and I suspect communally, and in ever-smaller circles. Here in America, for instance, rights seem to be precariously balanced on some weird precipice of power and (mis)information. So, yes, courage is needed.

But also, it takes balls and ovaries to walk away from arguments and conflict, especially where there's no peace in sight. We must cultivate the wisdom to fight when we can *and* to fold up when that's wiser. For changing course, admitting failures—or as I prefer to call them: detours—takes bravery too. And by not letting our egos get in the way, we can regroup and reemerge that much stronger.

The Courage of Retreat

What I've learned from Zelenskyy, and from this front-row seat we all have to a war between "good" and "evil"—or, more accurately, between those who are awake and those who've been asleep for eons—courage comes in forms other than just facing danger. In battle, as in life, it is sometimes necessary to retreat, and this takes tremendous guts and the relinquishing of ego.

Ukrainian forces tried long and hard, for instance— and at a very high human cost—to defend against Russian insurgency in the city of Sievierodonetsk—a strategically important Ukrainian holdout in the Luhansk Oblast in Donbas. The Sievierodonetsk-Lysychansk area in southeastern Ukraine was a beyond dangerous, constantly bombarded region that our man Ze nonetheless visited, showing his confidence and belief in his troops. Still, a time came when the casualties and the nonstop destruction called for another approach. "Remaining in positions that have been relentlessly shelled for months just doesn't make sense," said the governor of Lukansk Oblast, Serhiy Haidai, in June 2022, when Ukrainian troops were ordered to withdraw. "There is no point in staying . . . just for the sake of staying."

As war experts explained, strategically ceding territory can actually help to win a war. Knowing when to cede, knowing when to retreat, is as important as facing the fight head-on. *There's no point in staying just for the sake of staying.*

The Boldness in Being Human

Zelenskyy and the Ukrainian people have demonstrated that courage is just as necessary for our very humanness as it is for heroism. It takes the same bravery to change course as it does to withstand danger. It takes the very same courage to face up to our mistakes as it does to speak up against the wrongs of the world.

"Bravery is rightly believed the first of human qualities, as it guarantees all others," Zelenskyy addressed the Brave Ukraine fundraiser in the UK in May 2022. Life, with its many potholes, takes bravery just to live it—and it does so from the very beginning. Even as a child learns to walk, bravery must overcome fear—that's how any first step is taken. And trial and error, too, is plucky: standing, then falling, then trying to hold on to the wall or widening your feet, or . . . Course-correction can stem only from that first human quality of valor.

The opposite of bravery, on the other hand, is not only paralyzing, but can be extremely dangerous. In lacking it, you can't do what needs to be done—admit you were wrong, change direction, cut your losses—and that creates dire situations. The opposite of courage is a slippery slope toward calamity.

"It all came from cowardice," Zelenskyy said about the Russian invasion. And "when cowardice grows, it turns into a catastrophe. When people lack the courage to admit their mistakes, apologize, adapt to reality, learn, they turn into monsters. And when the world ignores it, the monsters decide it is the world that has to adapt to *them*."

These words of Zelenskyy's—this description of the lack of courage—is just as important as his admirable boldness in facing danger; his reminder that it takes courage to admit wrongdoing and to alter your path is every bit as brilliant. Because we have so many symbols of heroism and super-human strength in our mythology and storytelling—but do we have enough reminders that it takes courage to be human?

Every human being, every organization, every country makes mistakes, but it requires an immense amount of guts and the quieting of our egos to admit mistakes and to grow from them, lest we become the monsters Ze speaks of . . . or just really, really unhappy people.

Decisions

Take it from Ze: "Courage must be a criterion for evaluating decisions. Courage and practicality."

What is the brave decision here? Let's ask ourselves, and let us choose it, even if it doesn't seem Brave with a capital B (as in folding and changing course). Not to mention that courage looks different for different people. Remember the relationships example? Sometimes the brave thing is staying and working on one's love story or dream or project. Other times, you gather your guts and willpower to fold up and get the bleep out. Only *you* know which is the braver choice. And there are times when you think you don't know. But if you quiet the noise around you, if you get in touch with your Inner Zelenskyy—your own inner guide, the one with all the clarity . . . if you garner the spunk and the willpower to hear your own answer . . . well, you will hear it then. You will clearly feel which is the way of courage.

"It's okay to be afraid," as we now teach our children and ourselves. "Be afraid but try it anyway." Or be uncomfortable and keep going, discomfort and all.

Stop waiting for help, for the perfect situation, for more information, for lightning to strike. As Zelenskyy has shown us: be brave in the face of fear, and the help will come. We must be brave first, though, we must be brave regardless.

So give your dream a shot, ask for more responsibility (and a raise). Go all in, believe in yourself, try your hardest.

Or walk away, stop throwing good energy after bad. Quit your job. Do nothing for a while.

Bravely retreat . . . and then keep going. Leave it all behind and attempt something completely different.

Go on a date with someone who's not your usual choice. Fall in love. Resuscitate your marriage.

Leave him or her. Be alone. Be your truest self.

Just don't forget: courage looks different for each of us, and it does not depend on the opinions of others. To find out where your innate bravery is calling you, go within, connect to your Inner Ze. Ask yourself, *What am I afraid of?* And, *Where would courage take me?*

Decide with courage.

12

Be the Link

Peace in your country does not depend anymore only on you and your people, it depends on those next to you.

—*Zelenskyy to the US Congress on March 16, 2022,*
in a plea for help

The war in Ukraine, in conjunction with a global pandemic, clearly revealed that we are inextricably intertwined in this world of ours—no matter where we draw boundaries and create or buy into separation. The truth is, we really are all one, as esoteric as that may sound. We are one big, interconnected organism—much like a forest with seemingly separate trees is an unseen web of interconnected roots beneath the ground.

In pandemic/war times, the hidden web finally became visible.

And so . . . as Zelenskyy pointed out, you couldn't just isolate your state anymore and create peace there and live happily ever after. In our era, when another nation is in trouble, it affects you as well, like it or not. As he said in a speech to Australian universities, "For many countries, the time has come when their own interests must yield to the interests of the planet."

And so . . . while we don't usually walk around thinking of how connected we are to the entire planet (unless we're on psychedelics, maybe), calamities—as awful as they are—do us the service of highlighting this interconnectedness.

Our job is to pay attention.

Everyone's War

Time and time again, to nation after nation, Ze explained that Ukraine was not fighting just for the freedom and the livelihood of its own land, but for democratic values and way of life all over the world. That may sound like lip service at first, but it is a fact that becomes clear when you examine the region's history.

It's as if, while the modern world kept inching its way toward a vision of coexistence, Putin sunk deeper and deeper into a Russian imperialistic past. He even likened himself to Peter the Great when celebrating the czar-turned-emperor's birthday, comparing his invasion of Ukraine to Peter's "reclamation" of Russian lands from neighboring countries. What Putin didn't mention was the anguish the czar's conquests caused—including in the Baltics, which he coveted in order to gain access to the Baltic Sea (a beautiful sea it is).

Putin's imperialistic dreams may be rooted in old czarist beliefs, which are as outdated a vision as you can think of. Yet there he was, seeing himself as the Father of Russian Lands and stirring Russian nationalism within his citizens—and arresting those that spoke out against it. If such ambitions were not stopped in Ukraine, they would certainly creep on as far as they could go. And an expanded, imperialist Russia would pose a threat to everyone.

"You perceive our struggle for freedom as your own struggle," Zelenskyy addressed the parliament and "ordinary citizens" of the Republic of Latvia, "because right now, in Ukraine, the fate of all of us, all Europeans, is being decided."

What would stop Putin from trying to reclaim Latvia, Lithuania, Estonia? And those are just the Baltic states. South of them Belarus was already a Russian puppet of sorts; parts of Georgia had already been occupied by the Russian Federation. And then what about Moldova, Poland? And then, and then?

"There will be either urgent help for Ukraine, which is enough to win, or Russia's postponed war with you," Zelenskyy told the leaders of NATO countries. Because, when you looked at the situation holistically, it was clear that

Ukrainians were fighting and dying for more than just their homeland. The struggle here was for a progressive way of life that was enjoyed by most Europeans and coveted by many people born into less than free countries. Not to mention that this fight was also being closely watched by other autocrats who wanted to take over *their* neighboring countries.

In essence, Ukraine was defending the rights of every sovereign nation. "What happens in Ukraine matters to us all," as Boris Johnson put it.

Because "we defend ourselves against the onslaught of tyranny craving to destroy everything that freedom gives to people and states," Zelenskyy explained in a video address in May 2022. "And such a struggle—for freedom and against tyranny—is understandable for any society in any corner of our planet."

And it *was* understood.

And even when governments were slow with help, the bulk of human beings supported the Ukrainian struggle. For in some part of ourselves we understand that we are interconnected, that the yearning for freedom is a universal yearning, and that all people have a right to this freedom we so desire—as Ze himself pointed out on America's Independence Day, even quoting our Constitution. Over and over again, he repeated that the Russian aggression against Ukraine is aggression against a united Europe and against "our common values." These values are rooted in mutual respect, cooperation, and connection of all people.

Still, as time passed, Ukraine's struggle predictably lost the spotlight of the world—especially the attention of everyday folks who were far away from the battleground, like in the United States. Every country had its own issues to deal with, and the cost of supporting Ukraine in this war might have seemed too high to some. Which is why Zelenskyy's constant interviews and speeches and reminders were so important—so that we would also think of the cost of *not* supporting Ukraine. As he said almost six months in, "By protecting *our* state, we automatically protect everyone who has already been threatened or may still be threatened by a terrorist state."

And then right on the cusp of the "Victorious New Year," as Ze called it, he traveled to the US Capitol and gave a historic in-person speech to Congress. Speaking in English, he thanked Americans for their support.

"Your money is not charity," he said. "It's an investment."

Butterfly Effect

It can be difficult for us to feel invested in battles going on elsewhere, in struggles happening to others—until, that is, we realize that there is no elsewhere, there are no others. As Ze said after talking to US officials, "When democracy wins in one country, it wins all over the world." And in the meantime—in today's interconnected reality—its lack becomes everyone's problem.

So how does a war *elsewhere* affect us?

Of course, we all noticed the ridiculous prices at the pump—those were obvious, even in America. But the disruption of gas and oil hit Europe especially hard. It was their reliance, in fact, on Russia's oil and gas that caused some European countries to hesitate in supporting Ukraine. Because Russia was a huge producer of both—particularly to its neighbors—and as sanctions against its aggression kicked in, so did deficits. Then an angered Putin created false shortages, turning the nozzle off and on as he pleased. And it became a mad rush to ensure European homes could keep the heat on in the winter of 2022–23.

Combine this with a geopolitical reshuffling—more nations joining NATO and increasing their military spending, understandably spooked by Russia's belligerence—and the stability of the world became ever more precarious.

Plus, this full-scale war that began in early 2022 greatly disrupted the global food supply—the more so the longer it lasted. Both Ukraine and Russia had been major exporters of wheat, barley, corn, and cooking oil. But Russia's invasion broke that flow (on top of supply chain issues already caused by the pandemic). This meant inflation, shortages, and exacerbated famine.

Here's an example: Ukraine had been one of the world's largest contributors to the World Food Programme—the UN agency that provides food aid to nations in crisis; this flow had to be reversed in the war, with the WFP now needing to provide aid to Ukrainians.

"Who always suffers?" Zelenskyy asked at a British think-tank conference. "The poor. . . . We are sure that the middle class will also suffer."

"It is exactly such people, such companies, our Ukrainian

south that have guaranteed the world's food security," Zelenskyy also said after grain tycoon Oleksiy Vadatursky was killed by Russian shelling. "It has always been so. And it will be so again."

Furthermore, this war created the fastest-growing refugee crisis in recent history, with millions of Ukrainians fleeing to suddenly overburdened neighboring countries and millions more displaced within Ukraine. The bulk of these refugees were women, children, the elderly, and the disabled—the most vulnerable people, in other words.

No matter which way you looked at it, Russia was a bully wreaking havoc. It had more nuclear weapons than any other country in the world—and it was huge, with hopes of getting huger. Plus, it had viewed itself as an opponent of the West for eons—this ever-present conflict and competition was like part of its identity. More so, Putin was only one of numerous such view-holders; there were other anti-West autocrats watching his aggression and taking notes. And we had been reliant on autocratic "partners" for far too long. In the case of Russia, Europe's reliance on its oil and gas was the big problem . . . but also, wasn't it time for alternative sources of energy, anyway, and for everyone? This fight sure brought a lot to the surface.

So, yeah, you could say the Russo-Ukrainian war was everyone's problem—and not a small one.

Collective Trauma

Who always suffers? was the question Zelenskyy had posed about global conflicts.

There is no doubt that this war has created layers upon layers of pain that will affect Ukrainians for generations to come. So many of us—descendants of wars, persecutions, terror—know this in our bones, because that's where trauma remains. We need only look back a couple generations to understand the profound ramifications of genocide and of combat—and of how it's all carried in one's bloodline.

Still, it's difficult to imagine the trauma Ukrainian children have been experiencing. And we can but guess at its aftereffects.

The stress of war, the displacement, the separation—remember, by law, most men had to remain in Ukraine, apart from their fleeing children—literally changes people on a genetic, or epigenetic, level. For research has shown that the trauma experienced by our ancestors likely affects the way our own genes are expressed. So what Ukrainian children have had to endure affects not only them, but will be carried by *their* future children as well.

That's what Ze kept repeating—that the consequences of this struggle are more enormous than we can fully comprehend in the present; they will reverberate for years to come. And we, humans, are all affected. The fight for freedom is on!

"It's not just the moral duty of all democracies . . . to

support Ukraine's desire for peace," Zelenskyy said in an April 2022 video address. "This is, in fact, a strategy of defense for every civilized state. To put pressure on Russia as much as possible to restore peace and security as soon as possible. To restore the power of international law as soon as possible, and to prevent the catastrophe caused by the application of the law of force. The catastrophe that will inevitably hit everyone."

He kept telling us that as long as there were forces trying to control, overtake, and limit the sovereignty of other people, we were all in trouble. I would just add that this includes the sovereignty of the Russian people—even those who themselves do not care that their autonomy was taken from them a long time ago. Because "hatred must lose; freedom must win," as Ze said. "First in Ukraine and then wherever tyranny will try to raise its head."

And as he told the UN General Assembly back in 2019—while then dealing with only the war in Donbas—"In today's world, where we live, there is no longer someone else's war."

Self-Care as World-Care?

The idea of interconnectedness is far more encompassing than just the mayhem of geopolitics. It is actually the basis of our very existence as humans, for we can either lift ourselves up or burn the whole thing to the ground. And each person is a link in this chain of existence, whether we realize it or not.

In our own lives, when we understand how much we affect one another, we begin to operate with more kindness in the world . . . we disperse an ounce of goodness in every interaction—in our cars on the road, in our dealings in stores and offices—and this goodness then spreads little by little, even as countries and governments are still figuring it out. But we must also remember that this goodness begins within.

While we each affect the whole, the whole also affects us—and that's where self-care comes into play.

"Our task is to hold on, to take care of ourselves, including our emotions," President Zelenskyy told his people in a July 2022 video address. He was discussing the anxiety caused by living in war, where even periods of quiet feel strewn with approaching danger. But for those of us *not* living in a war zone, anxiety too seems to be at an all-time high.

As the world still grapples with the effects of the pandemic, much of Europe remains at the footsteps of the conflict in Ukraine and its fallout. In the US, we never know where the next massacre will take place. Climate change and its related natural disasters put every continent at risk. And on and on. . . . Still we must care for ourselves and hold on to hope. We can't let despair pulverize us into oblivion.

Even as we feel our intertwined roots more than ever, it is the job of each of us to keep ourselves together so that we can, in fact, affect the whole of the forest floor.

And the *how* is simple(ish):

- Remember that you matter—a root intertwined with all the other roots, you've got to take care of *you*. Tend to the goodness within you so that you can give it to others.

* Find activities that are meaningful, even if it's not through work that pays the bills; it can be volunteering; creative expression; caring for family, for an animal, for a plot of land.

* Take care of your physical self too: eat well (fun fact: according to a *Time* interview, Zelenskyy starts each morning with eggs), move your body, stretch, sleep, and so on.

* Connect to your center, your inner truth, your power. Plug into this power source daily (i.e., meditate, walk in nature, take breaks, breathe deeply, rejuvenate yourself regularly).

* Take your light out into the world with each interaction, each engagement, each external effort: smile at passersby, hold the door, pick up a piece of garbage, purchase a Ukrainian product, donate a few bucks, or just send good thoughts if money is tight. . . . In one way or another, be a mensch like our Ze!

* And when you have an off day—as we all do—get back up on the self-care/mensch course and keep going.

You may not be leading a nation through crisis, but you too are a powerful instrument, so treat yourself accordingly. Just as a lack of peace and goodness affects you, you get to contribute to that goodness and affect *it*. And when you plug your powerful energy into the whole, you have no idea how far your own goodness will go—for even a single match can light up a cave of darkness.

When you realize the interconnectedness of us all and take care of the instrument that is You, you can play your part as a link to the upliftment of the entire world.

So take care of this You. Do your best. Be the link.

13

Remember: The Whole Is Greater than Its Parts

We united as a nation, even though our people understood they would be outnumbered tenfold and there would be no way out, just no way out. We fought for our existence and for survival—that's the combined heroism of everyone, of the people, of the authorities, and of the armed forces. We became a single fist.

—*Zelenskyy in an April 2022 interview with* 60 Minutes, *when he was asked how Ukraine managed to fight Russia to a standstill*

President Zelenskyy intrinsically understood that unity was the secret weapon for Ukrainians' survival in a war in which their army was ridiculously outnumbered. That's why from the very beginning, he urged his people to unite against the Russian forces despite their great disadvantage—and he told them many a time that each person's effort for the cause, for Ukraine's very existence, was necessary. Each person was needed to overcome the struggle. Every one of them, in essence, became part of "a single fist."

Now, Ukraine, like the bulk of modern nations, was filled with discord, politically and otherwise. But at the most vital moment of its story, none of the differences mattered. Only unity could help the country withstand Russia's attack. Only unity made sense. For a collective will is that much stronger than each individual will within the collective—especially a collective will for good, for the rights given to us by God, as Ze had put it.

European Unity

One of the most unexpected things that happened in Ukraine upon Russia's full-scale invasion was, in fact, this unity in a previously disjointed government—unity between politicians who had only recently been warring among themselves, and a cohesiveness that was very much needed to withstand whatever was thrown at them. In the face of annihilation as a nation, their differences suddenly morphed into a joint mission to survive and thrive.

This Ukrainian cohesiveness was at the forefront when

the nation's government was working toward joining the European Union—that long-held dream of theirs—with a joint statement simultaneously signed by chairman of the Verkhovna Rada Ruslan Stefanchuk, Ukraine's prime minister Denys Shmyhal, and President Zelenskyy.

"Today we are signing a joint statement," Zelenskyy announced, "which is a signal of the unity of all branches of government and is evidence of our determination to achieve Ukraine's strategic goal, namely full membership in the European Union."

And when Ze addressed the European Council, months into his country's fight for its existence, he urged Europe to come together as well against the imperialistic force that sought to destabilize it. He similarly understood that Ukraine's victory would be that much faster with a united Europe. Not to mention, this same unity was necessary for Europe to thrive.

"It's time," he urged the council. "It is time for you to be not separate, not fragments, but one whole." Greater unity, he explained, had become the foundation of Ukraine's strength. "Everyone is working for one result—state protection, and thanks to this we managed to do what the world did not expect, Russia did not expect: Ukraine stopped their army. And everyone was afraid of it," he added. "Remember?"

Remember?

By uniting, Ukraine unlocked a power that is available to all of us, and it is based on the fact that the whole is greater than the sum of its parts—that while every person on their own can achieve only so much, together we can do great things. Working in tandem, the roots beneath the soil can bring back to life an entire forest.

Group Magic

Volodymyr Zelenskyy happens to be an only child—an only child who had to navigate many changes that he had no control over . . . until he was old enough to take control, that is, and to create comradery. And this makes sense, for aren't we all seeking whatever it is we might have lacked?

Shortly after Ze's birth, his father's work took his family to Erdenet, Mongolia (a place where numerous Soviet engineers lived in the eighties). His school years were spent back in his hometown of Kryvyy Rih, which he'd said was as a "city of bandits" then, in the shadow of a fallen USSR. But Zelenskyy's outlet of comedy and performance brought him from darkness to humor and, perhaps even more significantly, from aloneness to fellowship. His understanding of group magic was an inherent component of the many years he spent in the business of making people laugh.

Ze wasn't one of those solitary comedians—bombing or slaying on stage alone. From the very onset of his career, he came together with his friends to compete as a group in the Russian television series called *KVN*, "the club of funny and inventive people." He and his comedic buddies founded the national *KVN* team of Ukraine, which they called Kvartal 95, after a busy quarter at the center of Kryvyy Rih. This team eventually morphed into the Kvartal 95 Studio, which produced the very *Servant of the People* (among tons of other popular projects) that took Ze to where he is today.

Contrast creates context—and so from his solitary existence, Zelenskyy's yearning to collaborate emerged. On Kvartal 95's website, he's quoted as saying, "Our ambitious objective is to make the world a better place, a kinder and more joyful place with help of those tools that we have, that is humor and creativity."

It seems his goals were always a "we," never an "I," for on his path he had learned the power of the whole.

It was, in fact, collaboration that brought our man his great career success as an entertainer. He and his friends made a name for themselves poking fun at the very government of which he eventually took the reins. And when that moment came, he knew it had to be a group effort—a gargantuan one at that. Yes, he took the people he trusted with him into government—something he was criticized for—but he also brought in the experts needed to run a country, as he continues to do. See, his success was never based on his ego; it was founded in his understanding of group magic.

What Makes the Impossible Possible?

As we discussed in the previous chapter, interconnectedness means every part, every person, every action counts. Like Richard Branson said when he toured the destruction and met with Ze in Kyiv in the summer of 2022, "When it comes to supporting Ukraine, every effort matters."

Each little bit contributes to the whole.

This concept of millions of pieces making up the puzzle is one that Zelenskyy understood long before Russia began its full-scale invasion. In fact, he encouraged his people to seek out unity since first coming to power. He knew that a unified sense of Ukraine was needed for it to flourish.

In his inauguration speech, Zelenskyy reminded his people, "We all are Ukrainians. There is no such thing as less of a Ukrainian or more of a Ukrainian, the right Ukrainian or the wrong Ukrainian. . . . From Uzhhorod to Luhansk, from Chernihiv to Simferopol, in Lviv, Kharkiv, in Donetsk, Dnipro, and Odessa—we are all Ukrainians. We have to be united, and only then we are strong. . . ."

And as war raged full throttle, he repeated his wish, his prayer for his people. "Save us from strife and division. Don't let us lose unity. Strengthen our will and our spirit. Don't let us lose ourselves." He spoke solemnly from Ukraine's beloved Saint Sofia Cathedral on Eastern Orthodox Easter—a vital holiday for Ukrainian (and Russian) Orthodox Christians.

He constantly urged his citizens to look past their differences—religions, languages, ethnicities—and to come together in their commonality: their shared dream of a free, prosperous, European Ukraine. "Skeptics will say, 'It's a fantasy. It's impossible,'" he said when he was elected. "But maybe this is just our national idea: to unite and do something that's impossible, in spite of everything."

Many "impossible" things have been done throughout history; that's how we move forward as a species. But never have they been done single-handedly. Seriously, even for those folks who are seen as solo players—for each one who went down in the books for an impossible feat—many others had to come together in support of them. This isn't always an easy reality to accept—especially for us individualists going it alone—but finding or creating a shared objective with others is what makes the impossible possible.

Zero-Sum Bullsh*t

It is a law of life that when you come together as one, you are greater than the sum of your individual parts. And so the secret to our success as humans in the world is the same as the secret to Ukraine overcoming Russia: unity. And when, in fact, enough of the free world came together to support Ukraine, it became clear that the tyrannical forces of Putin would not win, that they would be defeated, however long it took.

Unity is our way forward—it is the only way, in fact, that we can ensure peace and opportunity for humankind.

As we face global challenges, our truest challenge will be uniting as a species—looking for ways to join together rather than to divide, seeing our very humanity as the basis of all people. And this is also the challenge within nations, within communities, within families.

So while we will need to reach a global tipping point where enough of us understand our oneness, our actual work begins on a smaller scale. We must each work for unity in our own lives. For in unity we overcome obstacles, we do the undoable, we become that single fist of triumph . . . but also, we have a helluva lot more fun. And this is an understanding we all eventually come to—hopefully while still kicking!

See, most humans are not as on-point when they're young as Zelenskyy was, realizing his brilliance shone brighter yet when combined with others. Many of us struggle and hustle to succeed in our chosen pursuits. Yet when we operate from a zero-sum mentality—the idea that in order for someone to win, someone else has to lose—we make things far harder on ourselves. Too much of our energy, then, is spent on comparing, competing, and trying to outdo one another. But unless we're playing a sport where competition is the aim of the game, all our competing and comparing is limiting our very success.

Society has taught us for far too long this zero-sum-game illusion. It is time to drop it. It is time to see beyond that veil and not be threatened by the success of another.

When we celebrate one another's wins, we learn from them. When we compete with no one but ourselves, we drive ourselves forward, conserving our energy for our very endeavors. When we collaborate with people, we make the world "a kinder and more joyful place," like Zelenskyy and his Kvartal 95 team aimed to do.

Let's look for opportunities, then, to nurture unity wherever we find ourselves. Let us encourage it within our families (anyone with multiple kids understands that challenge!), our businesses, our workplaces. Let us lend support to our fellows, even without personal gain. Let us share our secrets without fear of being usurped. And let us look past our differences, rather than looking for reasons to be resentful.

Unified Mysticism

On a mystical level, when we come together, our energy is that much more potent. Sometimes it's nothing less than pure magic. You know those experiences where a unified field takes hold—in meetings and presentations, classrooms and gatherings—when that inscrutable magic sweeps through the group and transforms the event, the hour, the moment into perfection. We've seen it in sports, performances, and, sadly, on the battlefield—when the many become one, operating as one organism.

As Zelenskyy explained to *60 Minutes* in the single-fist metaphor—and as research has proven—the focused energy of a collective is incredibly potent. For instance, numerous scientific studies have shown that when a large enough group comes together to meditate, accidents and crime fall in neighboring areas. . . . Can you imagine? We can literally reduce crime through intended group meditation. What else can we accomplish with unified intention?

There is no doubt of the effectiveness of a unified whole. Let us remember this in our everyday lives. Let us upgrade competition and comparison to collaboration and confluence. Let us foster unity and positive intention wherever and whenever we can.

Let us become a single fist for the benefit of all.

14

Peace Begins with You

Ukraine has united for peace. And for the sake of peace, it unites the world.

—*Zelenskyy in a speech to the European Council on March 24, 2022*

Peace is, perhaps, the most obvious and pressing goal of Zelenskyy and his people. And it sounds simple enough: the desire to live without war, the belief in creating rather than destroying, the vision of stability in which you can rear both children and dreams. It is the simplest of desires and yet one of the most elusive. Because while war is pretty much the opposite of peace, many other hindrances to harmony exist all over the world—as well as within our own lives.

Take a look at the United States, for instance, where our inability to control guns shatters peace in the most innocent of situations: in schools, at parades, in churches and synagogues and supermarkets. As Zelenskyy said in a virtual address to Stanford's 2022 graduating class after a school shooting in Uvalde, Texas, "Americans express condolences to Ukrainians over the deaths in war. And Ukrainians express condolences to Americans over the deaths in peace."

Except this "peace" is not full-fledged peace, is it?

While we are not at war with an external enemy, we are certainly at war with ourselves—a battle that mirrors the disharmony within our own lives and hearts. Because all of us, humans, have found ourselves in situations where we can either foster peace or contribute to discord. And we each have chosen discord more times than we'd like to admit—perhaps without even realizing it. Which is why learning from our man Ze can help us choose differently in the future.

All for Peace

"I want to remind you of our peaceful mission in Afghanistan, when, at our own expense, we Ukrainians evacuated more than a thousand people from this country," Zelenskyy told the UN Security Council in April 2022—referring to Ukraine's 2021 mission that continued even after Americans had left Afghanistan. "And it was the hottest phase.

But people needed help—and Ukraine came," he added. "We evacuated people of different nationalities, different faiths—Afghans, citizens of European countries, USA, Canada. We did not distinguish who needs help, whether these are our people or not. We saved everyone."

Ze was demanding more effectiveness from UN's Security Council—a council that absurdly included the very aggressor that was terrorizing Ukraine: the Russian Federation, which was able to block decisions about its own hostilities. He suggested steps that could actually help the Security Council work for peace, including proposing an office in Kyiv that could specialize in preventative measures. "If every time there was a need everyone in the world was confident that help would come, the world would be definitely safer," he said, telling the council that if it couldn't up its (nonexistent) effectiveness, "then the only option would be to dissolve yourself altogether."

Because "Ukraine needs peace. We need peace. Europe needs peace. The world needs peace." And he didn't see this peace as a luxury but as a right that belonged to every human being.

*   *   *

"I want to congratulate now all Muslims of Ukraine and of the world," Ze said on the eve of the Muslim holiday Kurban Bayram, as Eid al-Adha is known in Crimea, addressing "the Crimean Tartar people, especially." (Remember: Crimea had been a hotbed of Russia's aggression for years, with many native residents displaced.) He then wished them what he had expressed countless times and in countless ways to all his fellow Ukrainians—and fellow humans: a wish for "the rule of peace [to be] restored."

As Zelenskyy said, Ukraine united for peace—which became the highest goal of folks of all creeds, religions, and ethnicities. And for that same goal, Ze worked to unite the whole world, reminding each government, each organization he spoke to that their participation in peace was also necessary. As we saw in the previous chapter, unity requires the understanding that *each* of us matters. For everyone has the choice to elevate to a more symbiotic way of being with their earthly neighbors.

Unity is needed to make large-scale peace possible—a flow that takes everyone's participation, or at least enough of us making the commitment to peace above all else.

So how do we make that commitment, then? What does it take? Because aren't we all sick of the lack of peace by now? Don't we all want to make this world safer and more stable? The answer—the solution—asks of us that we choose peace time and time again, above our base wants and ambitions, as Ze has told us. Simply, we must put peace first, holding it up as the highest of goals.

Peace above Money

"Precious peace is worth more than anything, more than any diamonds, more than any Russian vessel in European ports, more than any barrel of Russian oil," Zelenskyy said in March 2022, pleading for European governments and companies to stop doing business in Russia at the onset of war—to stop paying Russia for *anything*, in essence, as all payment fed its war machine.

"Values are worth more than profit," he also told French officials.

Choose peace over profit, he kept saying.

For while most large companies have long operated with the bottom line in mind, the time had come to weigh that bottom line against its cost. The time had come to price peace and harmony—as cheesy as it may sound—above revenue, acquisition, and power.

The fact is—as we are seeing more and more clearly—*not* putting profit first is paramount for humanity to prosper. For instance, decreasing pollution and waste may cost more for corporations, but it is no longer a choice—it's a must. And pivoting away from money-as-God takes a serious shift in perception.

While every person and every company has the right to pursue their success, that right does not abdicate their responsibility to humanity, to the world at large. This shift in understanding is needed in people and in organizations alike—both within the boardroom and within individual minds and hearts. It may sound obvious, but it bears repeating over and over until it's a truth from which we all operate: there are many things more valuable than money!

Money, while needed to live in our current world structures—to feed, clothe, house our families—is only a form of energy that flows to and fro. So how much is really necessary for us to feel secure, to feel like our loved ones are cared for? How much do we need to hoard? Not to mention that money has its limitations.

I mean, look at all the Russian oligarchs rendered pariahs by Putin's war. Their wealth can no longer get them the worldwide access to luxury they've come to depend upon. For how they got this wealth—at the cost of regular citizens struggling under hyperinflation as the USSR disassembled—came to haunt them. Their collusion with a ruthless government, which brought them billions while everyday people could hardly afford food—well, let's just say it wasn't nice. And when that same government began (or continued to) break international law and to commit war crimes in Ukraine, the money it helped the oligarchs rake in was finally seen as dirty. For money at the cost of values is hollow.

Now, some version of these Russian oligarchs exists in all countries—there may even be a Russian oligarch within each of us. When we buy into separation and into that zero-sum-game mentality, making a buck and gaining power at others' expense doesn't seem like such a big deal. But as Ze reminded us, values are worth more than anything money can buy. And when we compromise these values in order to get more for ourselves, we compromise our inner peace as well as the peace of the world.

Peace above Ego

Just as we put peace above profit in order to cultivate it, placing peace above ego is equally significant—lest we blow it all because of our inability to see past ourselves. This is why time and time again, Zelenskyy said he is willing to sit down with Putin (whom of course he couldn't stand on a personal level . . . who could?). He was more than ready to put his own feelings aside for the sake of peace. In fact, even as Russian forces got ready to invade Ukraine, Ze tried to get Putin on the phone with no success. "Sit down and talk to me," he spoke in Russian a couple days later. "I'm free. . . . Sit down, talk, not with your thirty-meter tables," he said, referencing Putin's infamously long desk, which kept him at a distance from anyone he was speaking with. "I'm your neighbor, I don't need your thirty-meter tables, I don't bite. . . . What are you scared of?"

Shouldn't neighbors seek coexistence rather than subjugation?

As war raged on, as atrocities committed by Russian troops came to light, it became more difficult for Zelenskyy to keep his personal feelings at bay—pain clearly written all over his face when he visited sites like Bucha, where his people had been tormented and slaughtered by Putin's army. Still, "We must talk until this war is over," he said, "and grab hold of every such opportunity."

But the more brutality Russia unleashed on Ukraine, with cities indiscriminately leveled—kindergartens, universities, theaters, apartment buildings, and shopping centers—the less possibility for diplomacy remained. Dead children, their stuffed animals among the rubble, made talks seem impossible. Grief and anger roared in the heart of every Ukrainian. Zelenskyy knew this, felt it himself, but also understood that ushering in peace and stopping the carnage remained his duty.

"Yes we have to fight, but fight for life," he told the Associated Press in April 2022. "You can't fight for dust when there is nothing and no people. It's difficult, emotionally difficult. . . . No one wants to negotiate with a person or people who tortured his nation. It's all understandable. As a man, as a father, I understand this very well. [But] we do not want to lose opportunities, if we have them, for a diplomatic solution."

"I assure you," he had said when he was first elected president, even before a full-scale war was unleashed on his land—but *after* major losses were already sustained in Donbas—"for our heroes to stop dying, I am ready to do everything. I am certainly not afraid of difficult decisions, I am ready to lose my popularity, my ratings, and—if need be—I am ready to lose this post without hesitation in order to bring peace."

I don't know if he had realized how prophetic his words would prove, as a horrific war would go on for months in Ukraine, and trying to end it would prove exceedingly complicated. He would need to temper his own strong emotions, as well as balance his goal of peace with the will of the people who'd elected him—people who became less and less willing to give up any of the precious land they'd been defending with their blood, sweat, tears, and loved ones.

"It's like conceding a freedom," said First Lady Olena Zelenska. "Even if we would consider territories, the aggressor would not stop at that. He would continue pressing, he would continue launching more and more steps forward, more and more attacks against our territory."

"I don't see any willingness on their side to be constructive," as Ze put it. And yet, "[Russia] is our neighbor with a huge population. So after we de-occupy our country, one way or another, we would still have to live as neighbors."

"History is unfair, it's true," he had said when he was first elected. "It wasn't us who started this war, but it is us who will have to stop it."

And so it was.

Peace over Comfort

"We Ukrainians are a peaceful nation," Ze stated when the war began, "but if we remain silent today, we will be gone tomorrow." And this same seesaw is true in every country and in every life, even: knowing when confrontation is worth it—knowing when it is actually needed for long-term peace. Because "Ukraine needs peace. Europe needs peace. The world needs peace," Ze told the rather ineffective UN Security Council. Sometimes mobilizing for peace is a necessity. For it's not about rocking the boat but understanding when that boat has already been rocked—and *who* is actually doing the rocking.

"Ukraine has always sought a peaceful solution," Zelenskyy said in a video address. "Because we count everyone killed. Because every ruined family, every ruined home matters to us. . . . For us a person is priceless." Yet, as he often reminded world leaders, there can be no peace when one side—or one man—is absolutely unwilling to seek it. "I emphasize in all negotiations," he told his people, "that sanctions are needed not as an end in themselves, but as a practical tool to motivate Russia to seek peace."

And you know what? Europe did invoke sanctions, even sanctions that were extremely uncomfortable for Europeans—when it came to gas and oil especially. But the fact that employing Russia, that paying it, was financing its brutal war against Ukraine made the discomfort necessary. And the understanding dawned that perhaps economic consequences could "motivate Russia to seek peace." This wasn't about punishment but about practicality, as Ze explained. And it was also about integrity.

Even if you can't force a party that's imperialistic at all costs to choose peace, you can at least *not* support it in its aims. You can at least withdraw from contributing to its capabilities. And that is what brings us to personal responsibility—how can we, as individuals, use our energy for peace rather than for discord?

It Begins with You

If peace is held as the highest ideal, understanding when to speak out becomes easier—basically whenever peace is threatened for our fellow humans. And, honestly, this ability is already within each of us—it is in our very nature.

I know I'm not a confrontational person (I hate confrontation—it sucks and feels awful and uncomfortable, and I've ignored many instances where perhaps I should've confronted others). Still, when those who are weaker are subjugated in front of me, something other than myself takes over.

I remember when an old Soviet man grabbed my brother by the ear at the dacha in upstate New York where immigrants like me spent summers in the care of our babushkas. A bunch of kids, my little brother included, were innocently but loudly clowning around and the man hadn't approved—and in the culture he came from it was okay to put your hands on any child you felt like; it was okay, it seemed, for the bigger person to take advantage of his size. I was maybe ten years old at the time and faced this intimidating man head-on, telling him off as best I could, making him leave my poor brother alone. A power greater than me took over, which rendered my fear and discomfort irrelevant.

This ability revisited me on several other occasions, and now I trust that it will as necessary. It's as if an energy emerges that is greater than my weakness—all the mama bears out there know what I'm talking about. It is perhaps a droplet of the energy which emerged in and for Ukraine in its predicament.

We all have a natural instinct to defend peace when it has been broken—especially to stand up for those who need our help. So don't look for confrontation but do trust that altruistic instinct—a balance demonstrated to us by the peace-loving yet strong Ukrainian president.

On the other hand, when you *look* for reasons to battle, war is inevitable; when you look for reasons to be resentful, you find them. When you sow seeds of discord, you invite clashes into being.

Now, this does not mean you should be a doormat, but it does mean putting peace above ego. So that rather than fighting, sometimes you walk away—or you talk calmly with the intention of working things out. Rather than seeing people as your enemy, you see them as fellows with differences—even if these fellows' beliefs seem utterly insane. And when all else fails and peace is, in fact, broken, you set your ego aside and find how best you can help stabilize the situation.

Inner Peace

Putting peace first in relationships is as necessary a shift as it is for countries and for companies—or at least it's a shift that can make our lives smoother, contributing to the peace of the collective. It can help us avoid wars within families and marriages, as well as within communities. . . . "Would you rather be happy or be right?" as the saying goes.

Often, those closest to us are a mirror to the mayhem within us—they trigger us—not to mention, they have their own inner turmoil to deal with. When you put all these inner and outer struggles into one household, it can be hard to keep the peace. That's why each of us needs to do the internal work necessary to promote harmony in our own hearts, first and foremost, and to come back to it time and time again.

There are warring factions within us just like there are out there in the world, and our job is to listen to them, to acknowledge them, and to negotiate between them so they can coexist: the ambitious part with the homemaker part, the adventure-seeking you and the family-man you, the person with a thousand responsibilities and the one that wants to fly free as a bird. Journal, meditate on, create ways that these various factions can all be taken care of (though not all at the same time) and then watch what happens when you face the people in your life.

Peace within really does translate to peace in your sphere of influence, so do not leave out your most significant arena: yourself! Find a way to cultivate inner peace and you will benefit a hundredfold, as will those around you, not to mention the world at large.

Do your inner work while letting yourself off the hook more; let your friends and family off the hook. Choose to lay down your resentments. Create goodwill, rather than being part of the separation that causes us to live in the never-ending cycle of "us versus them."

Claim peace internally. Claim it in your relationships and dealings. Claim it for the world.

15

Micro/Macro Manifestation

You can't think of the global and close your eyes to the details.

—*Zelenskyy's speech to the UN General Assembly*
in September 2019

As we saw in the past chapter, the peace we seek in the world begins in our very own hearts. The love-versus-fear saga is one we experience on both the global and individual levels. These are principles Zelenskyy not only understood but skillfully utilized in his leadership role, as well as in his life.

Ze realized the usefulness of creating and of embodying the very thing you want to see in your reality, even if you start small. And he was keenly aware of how the micro affects the macro, trying to convey this understanding to world powers long before a full-blown war hit Ukraine.

As soon as he was elected president in 2019, Zelenskyy began alerting other leaders to the danger his own country was facing (with armed conflict in Donbas seething since 2014). More so, he tried to show these leaders how his danger was their danger—and how that war, no matter how removed it may seem, was a threat to the entire world.

"You can't think of the global and close your eyes to the details or, as it may seem, even trifles," he said at the seventy-fourth session of the UN General Assembly. "Because that's how the foundation for the two world wars was laid. And tens of millions of human lives became the price of inattention, silence, inaction, or unwillingness to sacrifice one's ambitions."

Micro War = Macro Danger

Now, I don't know about you, but I didn't hear Zelenskyy's 2019 speech to the UN until we were well into 2022—once a sort of proxy global war was already in full swing. That is to say, I'm pretty sure inattention to detail has been our overall choosing. But what Ze was trying to tell the powers of the world back then, and maybe even the rest of us, was that when something is awry on the micro level, it will play out on the screen of the macro.

"For any war today—in Ukraine, Syria, Libya, Yemen, or any other corner of the planet, regardless of the number of casualties—is the greatest threat to the entire civilization," Ze said. "Because in 2019, *Homo sapiens* still resolve conflicts by killing. Throughout its existence, humanity has been constantly finding new ways to overcome distance, transfer information, cure diseases. And only one thing remains unchanged: contradictions between nations and states are still resolved not by words, but by missiles. Not by word. But by war."

Now, this is a fact that not only *can* affect us as individuals, but does. When our collective ego is more precious to us than human lives—power is more precious than peace— we're in trouble. "Don't think that war is far away," Zelenskyy said, explaining that "its methods, technology, and weapons have made our planet not so big anymore. And today, the time I spent on the last paragraph is enough to destroy the Earth completely."

Mic drop, right?

"This means," he continued, "that each leader is responsible not only for the fate of his own country, but also for the fate of the whole world." And later, as the full-blown war raged in Ukraine, he told the *Time* 100 Gala that "every one of us is the leader of our time."

So if every one of us is the leader of our time and each leader is responsible for the fate of the whole world . . . then—as Zelenskyy has told us—every one of us is responsible for the fate of the entire world.

How is *that* for a power trip?

The fact is, we are each part of the collective, and each part can help shift it. Let us focus, then, on shifting it toward evolution—toward our growth rather than our demise.

Macro Change Starts Within

How do we change a world where war is the logical answer for some? A world that's at the mercy of any madman with a big weapon?

"If we once learned writing, mathematics, invented the wheel, penicillin and conquered space," Zelenskyy reminded us, "humanity still has a chance." How do we—each one of us, then, leaders of our time as we are—make the most of this chance? This shot to build a world "where you will be respected for deeds, not for nuclear warheads." A world with "a new human mentality where aggression, anger, and hatred will be atrophied feelings."

Most folks are certainly not personally responsible for the creation of nuclear weapons—or for any weapons—and for the risk that they pose. And yet we are each responsible, not just for our deeds, but even for the thoughts and energy we put forth.

Once we understand how we fit and feed into collective consciousness . . . well . . . in awareness lies our very capacity for change.

The fact is, we cannot, as a people, build weapons and expect peace—and this is not a matter of judgment. It's just that, simply put, what we create in fear creates what we fear. This is a law that operates like gravity, whether on a pebble or on a planet, much like the idea that what you venerate, you give power to. These are energetic principles that work whether you believe in them or not—like gravity.

So ask yourself: What do you worship, what do you venerate? Is it the rule of force and control—whether in the office or in a household—or is it the rule of freedom and flow? Do you put money, power, status on a pedestal or are you more interested in the intricate qualities of a person and in the way they interact with the world?

And what do you most value within yourself? Is it your joyfulness or your compassion, or maybe your ability to find common ground? Or is it your pushiness and your knack for hammering things into place?

Here's the thing: we each have forcefulness and flow within us. It's not that one is bad and the other good. But if we only respect, believe in, know how to get results with might—which is often at the expense of peace and stability—we are contributing to a collective that respects might over peace as well. Once we really get this, we can choose to operate differently. Maybe not all of the time, but enough of the time.

Align Your Energy

Zelenskyy instinctively understood what some of us have to meditate and study and search the world to comprehend: the importance of alignment. It is the principle that, as within so without, and that, if you want to create something on the outside, your work begins inside your own heart and mind (and within your energy body, if you ask me, though I'm not sure Ze would put it that way).

As he began his presidency, Zelenskyy knew all too well how badly the bulk of his citizens wanted to be part of the European orbit, how much they wanted to align themselves with the European way of life. Some even died in order to overthrow a leader who bowed down to Russia rather than co-creating with Europe. But Ze also understood how important it was for his people—and for any people—to align internally with their goals.

"Yes, we have chosen a [political] direction to Europe," he said in his inaugural address, "but Europe is not somewhere there, it's here [he pointed to his head]. And when Europe is here [he pointed to his head once more], it will come to our country."

That right there—those very words are the blueprint for any goal of your choosing: when the vision for what you want is clear in your mind, when you feel its life with your whole being, it will eventually externalize itself as well. And much like a great coach—Phil Jackson comes to mind—Ze leaned on this blueprint fervently and often. Similar to Jackson—who's been called the NBA's greatest coach of all time and who was known for his holistic, Zen approach to coaching—Ze led his people toward an internal vision of the thriving reality they yearned to inhabit.

In his inaugural speech, Zelenskyy also outlined a goal for better supporting Ukrainian troops who'd been defending the sovereignty of their nation since 2014. "I will do everything so that you feel respect," he said. "Adequate and stable financial support, housing, vacations after completing combat missions, rest for you and your families." He added, "One doesn't have to speak about NATO standards, one has to create these standards."

It seems that like Gandhi (and Phil Jackson!) Ze knew you must *be* the very change you wish to see somewhere out there.

Of course, his initial efforts to up the quality of life in Ukraine were cut short. For instance, the badly needed update to Ukraine's infrastructure turned into a distant dream amid leveled cities and destroyed roads and bridges. But his mentality, his understanding of embodying the very transformation you want to implement, will surely help him and his people rebuild the Ukraine of their dreams.

In the meantime, "Our task is to hold on, to take care of ourselves," Ze told Ukrainians. "Including our emotions," he added, "to help the country's defense as much as possible, to protect the state, as much as it will be necessary for our victory." Because nothing—not even the intensity of war—changed the importance of cultivating the energy within yourself that you want to see on the outside (self-care as world care!). Plus, if every Ukrainian completely lost it, who would be there to defend, to maintain, to rebuild their land?

"When Europe is here [he pointed to his head] it will come to our country," he had told them in 2019. And in war, he reminded them that to take care of their country, they needed to take care of themselves, of their internal states.

Be It

As an actor, Zelenskyy not only understood but experienced the power of embodiment—of taking the space, walking the walk, inhabiting the skin of the person you wanted to be. He played the president; he became the president—if that's not quintessential manifesting, I don't know what is.

He carried this sort of wizardry with him into his wartime leadership, talking about victory even when it seemed unlikely, telling Ukraine that while it *was* beautiful (before so much of it came under fire) it *will be* great. He cultivated a belief so strong that he became it, with every word, action, and khaki T-shirt he wore. He became it and he never lost the opportunity to help his people become it—to embody the spirit of a united, victorious, thriving Ukraine. And in watching them, many of us could see their future success, for the seeds of it were all there—the dignity, the bravery, the can-do-ness of a future great country.

Of course, there was much to overcome, and sadly, at great human cost—but *"Mi peremozhemo,"* he told Ukrainians over and over again—"We will win!"

Create It

Zelenskyy skillfully demonstrated the way to bring anything into being: first within yourself, then out in the world. And it's a principle we can each apply to our lives and to our endeavors.

What are *you* creating, what are you claiming from out there in the cosmos for yourself? If, say, you have a vision for your life that is based in love and abundance and freedom and empowerment, spend time daily cultivating that very state of being.

As Ze reminded his nation, whatever it is you want your existence to look like, you must see its possibility and create it inside yourself first.

Yes, you will still need to go through the motions of doing what must be done, but you cannot forget about your internal state. I mean, you can, but that will make everything so much harder—hammering things into place without first aligning with them always is.

Instead, get aligned with your vision without waiting for it to materialize externally and you're golden. And the *how* of this is something our leader has also shown us, through his first career—playing.

*   *   *

Comedy and acting are but a heightened state of play, of pretend. And we all deserve the space to play, whether we are actors, bankers, or utility workers—the space to pretend to be the people who already have what they want.

Wanna self-actualize? Well, what does an actualized person feel like, act like, think like? Embody that person the way Zelenskyy embodied an unusual, inspired president. Embody that person more and more until you become them.

And as for the world, as for the collective we all inhabit, ask yourself, "What am I contributing to the unified field?"

Because we all contribute something. And guess what—the more you are aligned with your personal vision, the more potent the energy you put forth into the world can be. For the aligned energy of one is more powerful than the haphazard energy of dozens. Again, just take a look at Ze and his level of influence.

Ask yourself these questions, and often: *What am I embodying? What am I putting out there?* And be honest with your answers. Because, listen, sometimes we all add crap to the crappery; sometimes we all put more fear into an already-fear-based existence.

But even as we speak, the collective is changing. Because everything is always changing. So your questions for yourself are about how you will contribute to this change.

Have a think; choose wisely. In awareness and intention lies your power.

16

Create Faith

Hope always wins—even under seemingly insurmountable circumstances.

—Zelenskyy in a video address on the eve of Passover
in April 2022

"He has no religion," a Russian critic said of Volodymyr Zelenskyy when Ze was elected president of Ukraine. And the critic was right—Zelenskyy was not a religious man. Of course, what someone perceives as weakness, another transforms into opportunity.

In having no religion, a person can discover wisdom in *all* religions. Without dogma, one can find room for truth.

The lack of religion in the hands of the right individual

becomes an invitation for creating one's own faith. And it was an invitation Zelenskyy accepted wholeheartedly in his role as a wartime president—a position which is a hopeless one or a hopeful one, depending on who's in charge.

Soviet Cynicism

Born a typical Soviet Jew, Volodymyr Zelenskyy was raised without religiosity (as were most Soviet Jews, with "Jew" on our passports but scant knowledge of the religion itself). In fact, the Soviet times in which Ze began his life—the ones his parents had always lived in—didn't allow for much observance of any kind. Seriously; it was not legal. Forced atheism was the lay of the land in the USSR, which is pretty bleak when it comes to cultivating trust, hope, and belief in the forces of good.

Cynicism, rather than faith, was the general belief system of the Soviet people—cynicism that is easy to comprehend when you are lied to and controlled by your government for eons . . . when you're stuck in a grainy black-and-white photograph while the rest of the world has long moved on to Technicolor. Cynicism, one could argue, is the only way of being that makes sense. Except faith—that belief in something greater than the oppressive system or era in which you find yourself—isn't based on what makes sense on the physical plane. It is not a derivative of logic and order. It spans far beyond any structures—which is why it cannot be controlled by them, nor can it be broken.

Throughout the war, Zelenskyy often pointed to Russian

cynicism as a detriment to any sort of agreement. For instance, when trying to negotiate a temporary cease-fire in order to create an evacuation route for residents of Mariupol, he pleaded "for the Russian side to consider this issue without cynicism and actually do what it says." Unfortunately, many attempts at creating a corridor were thwarted by continuing strikes from the occupiers. For cynicism, or a lack of faith, prevents people from trusting others and, thus, from being trustworthy themselves.

Without faith, it's almost impossible to overcome one's circumstances. With it, everything is possible.

An Opening

When you aren't indoctrinated with a religious belief system at birth, you get to create your own—which can either be a boon or a burden—your choice. When, like the optimistic Ze, you foster a belief in yourself, in your abilities, and in the abilities of your fellow men, that blank slate is certainly an opening. It allows you to respect the faith of all people and to mean it wholly, without thinking that what you've been taught is the right way or the better way or the only way to be "good." It allows you to see the possibility of goodness in everyone. And it enables you to call that goodness forth.

In watching Zelenskyy communicate with Ukrainians throughout the war—with sincerity, transparency, and with gusto—it was easy to get the sense of his admiration for them, whatever their religion, language, ethnicity, or any other category/box humans use to describe themselves.

In his nightly video addresses, Ze used aspects of various belief systems to bring everyone to the same place: faith in eventual victory—that internal state that was needed for the external outcome. In short, he didn't care what separated his people—only what united them. And he sought to unify them in the kind of trust he himself had cultivated—a confidence not based on a book or on a pedigree, but rather on the certainty that it will all be okay in the end.

"The main thing," he told viewers after four months of war, "no matter how difficult it is for us today, we must remember that there will be tomorrow." And he always believed that an eventual tomorrow would equal peace, stability, and victory.

"There will never be such missiles that can break the will of the people who believe in themselves," as he put it.

The Jewish Christian Muslim Spiritual President

On the eve of Passover in 2022, amid the kind of oppression that Jewish people commemorated overcoming, Zelenskyy reminded all of Ukraine that "hope always wins—even under seemingly insurmountable circumstances." He called the holiday "a holiday of liberation" and "a holiday of life," drawing parallels between an ancient struggle that was surmounted and the struggle his country was still dealing with.

Similarly, speaking from the holy Saint Sophia Cathedral on Ukrainian Easter Sunday, Ze said, "The great holiday today gives us great hope and unwavering faith that light will overcome darkness, good will overcome evil, life will overcome death, and therefore Ukraine will surely win!" And on the eve of Kurban Bayram, "a special holiday that teaches sacrifice and guides people to do good deeds," as he summarized it, he told the Crimean Tartar population that "the year will come when we will welcome each other in a free Crimea."

Zelenskyy never missed an opportunity to lean on the tenets of any one belief system as a source of hope for the current harsh circumstances all his citizens were facing.

"One can destroy the walls but cannot destroy the foundation on which the morale stands," he said from within the hallowed Sofia Cathedral, "the morale of our warriors, the morale of the entire country." That confidence, that hope, that faithfulness was strong within him. After all, he was the grandson of the sole surviving brother (out of four) of a Jewish family that perished in the Holocaust. He believed that, ultimately, good would triumph. And he infused his people with this certainty every chance he got.

"We will not wait for a miracle," he told them in a Christmas Eve address. "After all, we create it ourselves."

Mountains of Tanks

Zelenskyy is not a religious man—*everyone* has established that—but he is a man of faith, and his people are a people of faith, whatever their religion. Their morale is what counted in the war, whether it came from Christianity, Judaism, Islam, humanism . . . or, in fact, from their love of family, of country, and of freedom. The exact source of their conviction didn't matter.

Still, it was faithfulness that allowed Ukrainian soldiers to face the second most powerful army in the world—second only to the US. They were heavily outnumbered in every category: tanks, aircraft, personnel, rockets . . . you name it. While the Russian Federation had spent $61.7 billion on defense in 2020, Ukraine had spent less than a tenth of that—$5.9 billion (according to the Stockholm International Peace Research Institute). But what Ukraine lacked in might, it made up for in morale and faith. And faith, as Ze knew, could move mountains of Russian tanks.

All of the billions spent on Russia's arsenal did not change the fact that much of its military lacked confidence in their objective. And how could they not lack it? They came from a cynical society and were sent to someone else's land to conquer it at all costs—often at the cost of their own young lives. As Zelenskyy maintained throughout the struggle, their loss was but a matter of time.

Ze nurtured this faith even in the darkest days, and he worked hard to cultivate it within his country and in the hearts and minds of the entire free world. Surely in his human form there were moments of doubt, but he didn't let those doubts take hold—he certainly didn't let us see them. Instead, he bolstered confidence in the face of loss, and he kept his confidence in himself. He understood that if his people lost hope, Russia would win; hope, faith, morale—those were the bedrock on which you either walked to victory or threw in the towel if it were lacking.

Let us, then, follow Ze's lead.

Hold On

So many of us bob up and down, believing in ourselves, then not believing, back and forth, based on what happens externally, rather than cultivating a knowing that's deeper than the reactions of the outside world. But in the not-believing, in the lack of belief, we almost predetermine the outcome . . . and then at one bottom or another, we muster that bit of faith once more and begin our climb back toward the light.

If we follow Zelenskyy's example, though—if we hold on to hope even through the challenges—our victory, our success becomes inevitable. Sure, we still struggle, but even while we suffer, our hope and our knowing reduces our suffering.

As Ze has shown us, faith is a choice that asks to be made over and over again. Over and over, we use it to conjure a certain outcome from the Universe, leaving no room for anything but. In fact, anyone who has achieved any big, unlikely dream had to wipe from their minds the possibility of *not* succeeding. Remember? They had to invoke a belief in their own limitlessness. Can we use the same principles to bolster ourselves not just on the path toward big goals but during any hard time we're invited to overcome?

It is in faith that we walk toward the light, and when the light is nowhere to be seen, it is to faith that we surrender once more.

"Move, Mountain"

We live in an era when religion has become less and less of a factor in many of our lives. Which is fine—as we've already established, as Zelenskyy has shown us, a blank slate can be an opportunity. Let us not waste this opportunity, though, and remain in a state of cynicism akin to that of the Soviet Union. Let us cultivate and nourish our own brand of belief. We need it!

So what does faith *look like for you?* Ask yourself this question.

Does the word make you cringe in its unsophistication? Because there has been a divide established in which faith and intellectualism, for one, are held as separate—as if the latter precludes the former and vice versa. But as the brilliant Ukrainian president demonstrates, faith is not the absence of intelligence—nor is it the absence of humor and fun, for that matter. It is what allows you to be the truest form of yourself, whether as a comic, a leader, or an intellectual. It allows you to hold the understanding that who you are at your core is exactly who you need to be, that when you base your life in truth—in the calling which emerges from that very core—you've already triumphed.

So I will ask you once more: *What does faith look like for you?*

For me, it is based in the spiritual understanding that God Is. That all existence is of a divine source, and that once we feel that source within ourselves, we can see it in everyone and everything around us. Not all of the time, of course (because, human), but enough of the time. So as we get pulled away from trust and from our own divinity, that understanding of is-ness—of God-is-ness—allows us to return: to return and lay down resentments, to return and forgive, to return and replenish ourselves enough to go back out there and seek and spread light, even amid the darkness . . . perhaps especially then.

That is what I believe—that is *my* faith. And I urge you to find yours. For in the words of Jesus, "If you have faith the size of a mustard seed, you will say to this mountain, 'Move from here to there,' and it will move; and nothing will be impossible to you." And in the words of Zelenskyy, "One can destroy the walls, but can't destroy the foundation on which morale stands."

May we each foster faith, then, whatever it may look like or feel like for us, so that we can move whichever mountains need moving. And may we all come back to our belief time and time again, so that our morale remains strong no matter what is happening around us. No one can destroy the depth of morale . . . for faith the size of a mustard seed can withstand Russian tanks and personal calamities alike.

17

Use Your Energy Wisely

No panic. We're strong. We're ready for anything.

—*Volodymyr Zelenskyy in a February 24, 2022,*
video address

In watching Ze throughout this stupefying conflict, many of us have had similar thoughts, worries, and queries about him—this hero, this superman who claims to be ordinary.

"Who is this comedian? This steel that is Ukrainian?" sang Five for Fighting in his tribute song "Can One Man Save the World?" And in a video where he's accompanied by the Ukrainian orchestra in front of the destroyed Ukrainian plane *Mriya* (the world's largest cargo plane that

Putin targeted on day one), he bellows, "But he's got every-one thinkin' / Yeah, he's got all of us thinkin' . . . Can one man save the world?"

The man the song focuses on is, of course, Zelenskyy, who, like the plane *Mriya*, represents the unbreakable Ukrainian spirit. . . . Yet the question still beckons:

How?

How could he *not* break under the weight of it all?

Day after day, in video after wartime video, as the world watched in admiration, Zelenskyy showed up. Some days he showed up exhausted, and other days he was spright-lier. Sometimes he was deadly serious and, other times, the twinkle in his eye was unmistakable—even in the somber state of it all. In a gazillion speeches; meetings; courtesy calls; messages to his people; talks with his generals, strate-gists, injured civilians, and soldiers, he showed up. And not only did he show up, but he gave it his best.

"The longer the war lasts, the harder it is to compete for the attention of hundreds of millions of people in different countries," Ze said. "But I will do everything possible so that attention to Ukraine does not fade."

And so it was—as we've taken to saying.

Still, we are brought back to the question of *How?* How did he do it all, even when there was no end in sight?

The answer: eggs every morning. "Invariably eggs," as Simon Shuster reported in a *Time* profile of Zelenskyy.

Humanness

Ze used his energy most effectively by simply being exactly who he was (and maybe the daily eggs helped?). It's as if he had figured out a long time ago that by inhabiting oneself fully and by letting go of pretenses, you're able to play to your strengths and to be the most productive version of yourself.

Zelenskyy did give a ridiculous number of speeches weekly—an amount which would be absolutely undoable for the vast majority of humans—but clearly, communication is his unique gift. And I would daresay it is a gift that reenergized him when he had such a high purpose for it—the saving of his country. He is a lifelong performer who can clearly handle the spotlight, and so by using his very strength to keep the world's attention on Ukraine—by doing what was natural to him—he expended less energy for more effect.

He also made full use of the tools he had available to him—ones many of us honed in the pandemic days: social media, combined with videoconferencing (see: he really is an everyman). Having already used social media to connect to Ukrainians in his run for the presidency, it helped him remain a "simple person" who spoke directly to them in war. And the constant videoconferencing allowed him to reach leaders, governments, festivals, and award shows without leaving his barricaded office in his besieged country.

Zelenskyy was perhaps the most vocal and transparent of leaders, remaining very much in tune with his humanity and, thus, with the humanity of all those he was speaking to and for.

When he first won the presidency, Ze told his voters he will "stay a human being" and not become a typical politician. After all, he was elected as "just a simple person who has come to break down this system." Later in the war, he again repeated how important it was to remain human. "You can lose your humanity and I want not to lose it, I want to keep my humanity," he told *60 Minutes Australia* in reference to getting emotional, to "showing weakness," as the interviewer put it.

"Getting used to war, it's the worst habit," he added.

By doggedly holding on to his humanness—his empathy as well as his humility, i.e., not giving in to the megalomania that envelops so many leaders—he remained an ordinary superman. It was this very ordinary extraordinariness of his that allowed him to work tirelessly for the people he was tasked with helping.

Shared Mission

Ze's vision and important work on behalf of Ukraine was very much shared by his life partner, his wife, Olena—a former scriptwriter for Kvartal 95, and the mother of his two children. She helped humanize Ukraine's plight with her own role—not just as a First Lady but "as a daughter and as a mother"—which is how she began her speech to the US Congress, similarly addressing senators not just as "politicians and party representatives" but also "as mothers and fathers, grandmothers and grandfathers, daughters and sons."

Mrs. Zelenska traveled to America to speak directly to Congress in the summer of 2022—a rare occurrence for a foreign first spouse. Yet, with both dignity and emotion, she told officials about Ukraine's innocent children, lost to Russia's war. "This girl is Eva. She liked to draw pictures. She was only five," she said, with a photo projected behind her of Eva's little body in the rubble. "Lisa was only four years old. She's no longer with us. Here is the stroller of Lisa.

"Russia is destroying our people," Mrs. Zelenska said, asking for more support to help protect those who remained. Her realness and clarity were a boon to the Ukrainian cause, earning her a thirty-second standing ovation from Congress.

The next day on the *Today* show, when asked if she worries about her husband, Mrs. Zelenska said, "No. . . . I know that he will be safe, I am confident that he will be safe, and he must stay strong because he inspires so many people and he encourages the entire world."

Perhaps it was *her* strength that was her husband's superpower. . . .

No Pretense

If we dig deeper for a silver lining to the great suffering—the tests that we endure here on earth—often the best in people comes out during those toughest of times. For instance, in America, those of us who lived through the days marked "before" and "after" by September 11 will never forget the mix of grief and comradery that enveloped New York City in its darkest moment. And the bravery, strength, and grace of the Ukrainian people in the wake of unspeakable atrocities will be remembered forever. Not to mention the sheer superhumanness that our human hero continually embodied in wartime.

And one of the coolest parts of this superhuman human was that at the onset of war, he completely dropped whatever pretenses he had left. I mean, it's not like he had ever pretended to be some bigshot politician; he was but ordinary, as he said more times than we could count. But with full-blown war, there wasn't even energy to waste on proper attire.

"Doesn't he own a suit?" an American official quipped after Ze's first speech to Congress. And, obviously, he did. But his energy was so precious at that time that preparing and donning a suit was absolutely needless and irrelevant. He had been marked a dead man walking by Russia, which was set on erasing the nation of Ukraine.

The rest of his government immediately dropped that suit act as well. No time for neckties; there was a country to be saved.

A suit did not make sense.

What did make sense in that situation was wearing simple fatigues—swapping a T-shirt for a sweatshirt here and there. What made sense was wearing Ukraine's predicament on his sleeve—which is why Ze stuck to his wartime garb even months later when speaking in Washington and then in Europe. Even with world leaders in historic places. Even with a king, even in a castle. Even still.

*   *   *

Doing what makes sense—dropping all pretenses, being exactly as you are in the moment—not just internally, but externally, openly, blatantly . . . well, that conserves your energy greatly. And it lets you be the brand, the very message you want to convey to others. You think less of what you *need* to be and you just be what you are.

Ze's iconic green T-shirt, as he is surrounded by officials in suits—it became a symbol of courage and of resistance, as well as of his ordinariness. He stayed a human being like he had promised, which made him that much more relatable to his people and to people all over the world. He wore his "everyman" with gusto and with gallantry.

He stayed true to the moment.

Fortitude

"No panic, we're strong, we're ready for anything," Zelenskyy told his people on the day war began. "Nobody is going to break us; we're strong, we're Ukrainians," he vowed to the European parliament a few days later.

It's as if he were calling forth the very mental fortitude necessary to withstand what was happening to his country— and he was calling it forth for all Ukrainians.

For himself and for his nation, Ze cultivated a strength, a faith, a belief that would withstand Putin's attacks and terror and eventually lead to Ukrainian victory. "Strengthen our will and our spirit. Don't let us lose ourselves," he invoked in the Sofia Cathedral in Kyiv. And along with fostering a strong morale, he understood the importance of taking care of his—and his people's—energy. He knew how important it was for *all* people.

"Every day you should not just ask yourself another question, but be sure to find the answer," he instructed the Stanford University students he spoke to on their graduation. "'Who matters most and why?' This is the main question for me: Who matters most and why?

"Take care of yourself," he told them, "your family, loved ones, friends; take care of the world."

Because this world of ours does need care, as do its inhabitants. But the thing about the strange modern era we live in—busy, stressful, and worrisome, even for those in war-free nations—is it can be extremely challenging to *not* leak energy to and fro, so that there's nothing left to give.

We lose our energy constantly, as we scroll through our phones and computers, grim headline after grim headline—or, say, when we get stuck in a social media vortex, comparing and contrasting and feeling not so great afterward. All day long our precious energy trickles out of us as we don one mask or another, pretending to be grander or more competent or something other than what we are. And again when we beat ourselves up for our mistakes and shortcomings.

So much of our lives are spent doing everything but the stuff that would bolster us rather than deplete us. And then we wonder why we have so little left in the tank. We chalk it up to aging and go on with our less than aligned lives.

Is there a better way? Yes. And isn't it poignant that a superhuman human showed us this way amid a damned, bloody war? There are lessons to be ingested here. For our energy is our currency. Let us use it, then, as deftly as Zelenskyy uses his.

5 Superhuman Energy Hacks from Our Ordinary Human:

1. <u>Play to your strengths</u>, your own unique specialties that give you energy even as you work your butt off. And make use of the tools you've got at your disposal—both the internal and the external ones, i.e., don't damn the megaphone; use it! Ze uses social media as an elevation tool, for example—it helped him greatly in becoming president in the first place. . . . Also, lean on your partners, your helpers, your community who support your cause—don't try to do it alone; remember: Ze's wife was a pillar he too leaned on.

2. <u>Drop all the pretenses</u>. The busier you get, the more that is asked of you in this world, the less energy you've got to spend on being what you are not. But you need not wait for dire or for peak life situations to drop the pretenses. Stop leaking your juice today. Why waste energy on shoring up some kind of facade? Who cares? Let them see you in your version of the plain army tee. Be your free, simple self.

3. <u>Stay connected to your cause</u>. Whatever your goal, bring yourself back to its origin. The *why* of it all. For Zelenskyy, it's been important to not lose his humanity, to not get used to and jaded by war, but to remember the very humans he was working for. Similarly, whatever our mission, we can bring ourselves back to it over and over, rather than getting lost on the treadmill to success. Stay connected to that yearning to serve, to advance, to create, to build, and it will feed you on your journey.

4. <u>Keep the faith</u> and have confidence in yourself. Sometimes your road can feel easeful and other times it seems fraught with potholes and obstacles. Remember that the faith of a mustard seed lives deep within you, regardless of how things are looking at the moment. It's that belief in ultimate victory, together with the belief in yourself and your ability to persevere, that will ultimately get you there, and that will give you all the energy you need.

5. <u>Take care of yourself</u> and your needs, even when it seems you don't have time for it. Self-care can be as simple (and as quick) as checking inward and bolstering your mood with a kind word to yourself . . . as simple as taking a moment to ask yourself how you're doing and to breathe a little deeper, or to take a break, a walk, a meaningless or meaningful chat with a friend. Finding ways to calm your anxiety is imperative on your path, wherever it may lead. Finding internal peace is imperative for creat-

ing it externally. And, also, the physical aspects of taking care of yourself: whether it's morning eggs and/or regular exercise, some decent sleep, and a vegetable or two—all of it matters. All of it is about filling your energy tank in order to have the very energy necessary for anything and for everything.

18

A Call to Power (and Responsibility)

Every one of us—everyone—is the leader of our time.

—*Zelenskyy's video address for the* Time *100 Gala in June 2022*

If there is one lesson that Volodymyr Zelenskyy imprinted in the minds of his people from the time he became president, it's that each one of them (like each one of us) has the opportunity *and* the responsibility to create the very circumstances they dream of. He aimed to break through the cynicism that was long embedded in descendants of the

Soviet Union—and, perhaps, in much of humanity—that makes people feel impotent and irrelevant.

Over and over again, Ze said otherwise.

In his inaugural address in 2019, "Every one of us is the president now," Zelenskyy told his people. "Not only 73 percent of Ukrainians who voted for me, but all 100 percent . . . It's not mine, it's our common victory . . . And it's our common chance for which we take shared responsibility."

Because that is the reality of empowerment: great power, along with great responsibility, hand in hand.

Self-Importance (The Good Kind)

"Now, imagine the headlines," Zelenskyy addressed the Ukrainian people. "'The President Does Not Pay Taxes,' 'The Intoxicated President Ran the Red Light,' or 'The President Is Quietly Stealing Because Everyone Does.' Would you agree that it's shameful?" he asked. "This is what I mean when I say that each of us is the president," he continued. "From now on, each of us is responsible for the country that we leave to our children. Each of us, in his place, can do everything for the prosperity of Ukraine."

These powerful words were not really heard by the rest of the world until Russia unleashed its destructive plans upon Ukraine, but they have been some of the precious gems that we've uncovered in the destruction—wisdom that can, in fact, change the world.

For how many of us take full responsibility for our

behavior and the way it affects the whole—the way it may affect the very world we leave to future generations? How many of us treat ourselves with the importance of the president? And I'm not talking about the importance based in ego here, but the accountability that Ze gently placed in the lap of every Ukrainian—the accountability, in fact, that lies in the lap of every global citizen.

Most of us run around in our lives not really considering the importance of our own actions. And it's not because we are bad people, but rather because we are not aware of the great power that lies within. We don't consider ourselves as very important, so how could our actions be? And we don't consider ourselves capable of affecting our own existence, not to mention the existence of our neighborhoods, our countries, the globe.

Incidentally, it's when we realize exactly how great and how powerful we are that we become accountable to ourselves and to the world for what we bring forth. We stop doing something negative "because everyone does," as Ze jokingly (not jokingly) turned into a pretend headline for the pretend president that he told every Ukrainian they were: "The President Is Quietly Stealing Because Everyone Does." But isn't that exactly how so many of us justify less than great choices? "Well, everyone else does this, so . . ."

In fact, it's how we make many of our choices—by looking to others.

Yet what Ukraine's president has shown us is that we can each take the leadership role of doing what *we* believe is right—even if we are only leading ourselves.

We need not look to the less-than-great or ineffective or uninspired behavior of other people to make our move. We can follow the inner compass that sits within us—the one we recognize when we actually stop copying one another and stop listening to all the external cacophony.

This internal voice will tell us exactly how it is . . . and we are always welcome to take its advice; and sometimes we may ignore it. But at least, then, we are making informed choices rather than following the often confused herd. We are putting stock in ourselves.

Internal Alignment

Volodymyr Zelenskyy long espoused the power of internally lining up with whatever it is you want to bring forth in your life or in the world. "A European country starts with everyone," as he had said. "And when Europe is here [he pointed at his head], it will come to our country."

This internal alignment that Ze literally pointed to is not just vital for the creation of our dreams, but also for leading a life where we truly become our own masters, regardless of forces that tell us otherwise. Because these forces, this amalgam, is beyond confusing without a compass of our own.

Oh my gosh, can you imagine if Zelenskyy listened to his critics, for instance? "In over his head," "weak," "clown," and so forth. As we now know, he was none of those things, not even close. But the important part is, *he* always knew it—he always knew who he was and what he could do. For it is within our own walls of bone and flesh where our great ability resides. And in that mastery, in that internal leadership, lies everyone's Ze-level magic.

From Internal to External

Now, making decisions for yourself is not to be confused with *not* listening to those who matter to you and not taking others into consideration—especially in a position of leadership. Actually, once you have listened to yourself and you've chosen your own path, you can even better consider the needs of others—and you can fold them into your path, rather than vice versa. That was very well orchestrated by our man Ze when he was coming to power.

First he established his core beliefs and chose to pursue being a Servant of the People—ignoring critics and doubters. Then he took to heart what those very people he was to serve wanted to see happen in their country.

Ze had spent years lampooning politicians and social conditions in Ukraine (and, FYI, when he included an off-color joke about Putin in his show *Servant of the People*, the show got canceled in Russia). Ze's production company, Kvartal 95, openly supported the Revolution of Dignity and Ukraine's freedom. It donated money to the war effort, and the group visited and entertained soldiers on the front lines in Donbas. Still, Zelenskyy didn't really have a platform of his own, which was one of the biggest criticisms hurled against him. But because he had a vision and was aligned with it—the goal of actually serving the people—he was able to use this "weakness" to support his goal. He and his team crowdsourced ideas from his large following!

Ze's supporters said the future president sought to know how the public desired to be governed before telling the public how it *should* be governed. One of the main tenets of his political platform, which was released in late January 2019, was to make strong use of public referendums, particularly via the internet, to determine the government's agenda and direction.

So he followed his inner compass *and* he asked the people what they wanted.

He created a symbiotic relationship where he embodied the needs of his citizens, while leading them toward being the best citizens they could be. As he told the *Guardian* in 2020, "The president can't change the country on his own, but what can he do? He can give an example."

And Ze proved to be a capable model for Ukrainians. "You are a great example for us, for the nation and for the whole world!" posted Kalush Orchestra on social media after winning the 2022 Eurovision song contest.

"We are looking up to you and we will do everything for the victory of Ukraine."

For Zelenskyy helped those he led understand the importance of their own inner compass—their moral guidance, their own Inner Zelenskyy. He placed upon all Ukrainians the power he himself attained—the power of the presidency—which turned into an unbreakable resolve in Ukraine's darkest hour. And for his part he took on a balancing act of being both the ship's captain and its passenger—since we are all passengers on the sea of life, even as we direct the boat to hopefully weather the storms.

Unpleasantries

Ze formed his platform around the platform of the people. He took his cues from them—their desire to be more Western, liberated, liberal, and global. He didn't make up these ideals, but he strongly agreed with them himself. And he held up these collective ideals as Ukraine's shared dream.

By the time Ze took the reins of his nation, the nation had already declared its goals (remember the Revolution of Dignity?). He simply helped his people understand the need for alignment, i.e., *when Europe is within them, it will come to their country.* And when war struck, he helped them cultivate the faith they needed to overcome it, as well as encouraging them to take care of themselves and their energy.

He was the captain of a boat in turbulent seas. And he did his job impeccably.

And sometimes his job sucked, let's be honest. Not only did he deal with daily tragedy at the hands of Putin's army, but he also had to do unpleasant things himself—as do all people, of course, in positions of responsibility.

He had to let go of governmental officials who weren't fulfilling their duties, for instance—or perhaps were even sabotaging the efforts of Ukraine's fight for its life (some of these people were his longtime associates, including a child-hood friend). In the summer of 2022, he announced that hundreds of criminal proceedings were taking place in regard to treason and collaboration with the Russian invasion. This included "the transfer of secret information" that officials suspected allowed Russia to easily capture large areas of southern Ukraine within a week of the war. And he let go of yet more senior officials amid corruption accusations in early 2023.

Being a leader meant facing the fact that there were people who betrayed Ukraine, even as others were giving their lives for it. And this was to be expected, in fact, in a land with strong ties to Russia. More so, this was to be expected in a former Soviet republic where people had learned to solely look out for themselves "because every-one does."

Now, the bulk of the Ukrainian people *were* loyal, prob-ably beyond the level of loyalty most citizens feel for their countries nowadays. But there are always outliers. And in this case, the outliers helped themselves, or they helped the country which they believed would win. It wasn't a matter of principle but a matter of personal benefit—or so they thought.

In other words, without a solid inner compass—that moral clarity we've been talking about—it's easy to lose our principles, our values, and to end up adrift, usually to our own detriment and to the detriment of the whole.

Zelenskyy and the majority of Ukrainians were risking everything to build a land of freedom and opportunity. But freedom also comes with great responsibility. That is what our man Ze reminded anyone who would listen—that it was time to rise to the call.

And so it was.

From Victim to Victor

We live in imperfect times (we always have). But even so, we each have a level of agency—no matter how crappy our circumstances may sometimes be. And as Zelenskyy told his people, in that agency we have the power to affect our lives, our communities, our world.

So many of us get lost in the victim role that life thrusts upon us at one point or another. It is understandable; hardships are . . . well, hard, and, for some people, the hand that they've been dealt is particularly brutal. Still, no matter how life has victimized you, remaining a victim is only a disadvantage. At a certain point, the one choice that makes sense is reaching for the very power of which Volodymyr Zelenskyy was reminding his people when he got elected president: the ability to affect our existence. It is a power that is both emboldening and terrifying.

"Our deepest fear is not that we are inadequate," spiritual teacher Marianne Williamson wrote in her book *A Return to Love*. "Our deepest fear is that we are powerful beyond measure." Because on some level, we all know that with power comes responsibility. And once we know it, we can't unknow it.

"It is our light, not our darkness, that most frightens us," Williamson wrote.

For once you find your light, there's no going back. Once you find it, you know that you can fix your life, however long it takes. You know that you can, in fact, contribute to the betterment of your world. You know that *you* are your leader and prophet and savior. And everything you do and everything you say matters.

This is a lot to carry, no doubt. Yet it is a much more useful weight than resentment and regret and any other of their companion emotions. And you can step into this hefty power of yours little by little, as slowly as you want. Just remember—in the words of Ze: "Every one of us—everyone—is the leader of our time."

19

One Brick at a Time

"I am confident that we will be able to rebuild our state quickly. Whatever the damage may be . . ." Zelenskyy *said in a video address in March 2022.* *"It will be a historic reconstruction. A project that will inspire the world just as our struggle for our freedom. Just as our struggle for our Ukraine."*

The reality of war is so brutal, it's difficult to believe that anyone would choose it—would launch it for any reason whatsoever. And yet it is a reality that was thrust upon Volodymyr Zelenskyy's nation, no matter how much he wanted to prevent it. It was thrust upon an entire people who would have chosen otherwise if they'd been given a choice, and on an entire land, with its beautiful old cities and vast, sprawling farmlands.

War was thrust upon Ukraine and Ukraine had to deal with it, like it or not. And in this way, Ukraine's ordeal mirrored all of the tragedies that happen to anyone on a personal or global level. But what Zelenskyy and his people have also shown us so gracefully is resilience. The patient resilience needed to begin again.

Destruction

The scope of the destruction caused by Russian attacks was massive, not to mention the loss of life—destruction that was as overwhelming as it was tragic. But everything would be rebuilt, Zelenskyy told his people, "whatever the damage may be," noting that a special state program for reconstruction would be created for every affected city. "The best architects, the best companies, the best projects. For every city!" he vowed. And he repeated this sentiment often because, unfortunately, it was often necessary—like when Russian forces destroyed yet more universities in Mykolaiv. "We will definitely rebuild everything they destroyed," Zelenskyy proclaimed. "Each of the two thousand educational institutions: every kindergarten, every school, institute, and university."

Zelenskyy needed his people to know that no matter how overwhelming the destruction, the country could and would handle its reconstruction. As needless and oppressive as it was, as dark and hopeless as it looked—buildings, bridges, even entire cities turned to dust and rubble and husks of cars and of life—he wanted Ukrainians to know that brick by brick, it would be rebuilt. He needed them to believe that life could and would return there. The whole world needed this belief, in fact.

It's not that Ukraine's president was able to eradicate the understandable fear and overwhelm of his people. It's that he needed them to see and feel past this fear. Ironically, it's an old Russian saying that comes to mind here: "While the eyes fear, the hands do." Ze was assuring Ukrainians that their collective hands would do what needed to be done, regardless of how scared or traumatized their eyes were.

Perhaps, coming out of the mouth of someone else, promises of rebuilding it all (and better) would have seemed like mere air, but from the mouth of Zelenskyy, they were vows of steel. And as much as humans have gotten used to dismissing what politicians say, Ze was not a politician. In essence, he was a builder. From scratch, he had built a lucrative performance career, then an entertainment empire, then an entire political party. When he said whatever needed to be done would be done . . . well, in the least, we knew he'd give it his all.

Reconstruction

Destruction—especially the destruction of war—occurs in sweeping bursts of anger, whole structures toppled in seconds, whole lives and worlds snuffed out as quickly. Yet anything that is created and built anew takes planning and effort and labor and time. A cruel paradox it is that something (whether a building or a relationship) that takes hours upon hours to build, takes only moments to destroy. And yet a step-by-step, long-view mentality allows us to climb out of any hole, rebuild any ruins, and withstand any trials.

After Russia launched its large-scale offensive in the eastern part of Ukraine, Zelenskyy told his people, "No matter how many servicemen get thrown there, we will fight, we will defend ourselves. We will do that every day." And it really was remarkable how for months on end, with no break in sight, the Ukrainian army defended their land. "We won't give up anything Ukrainian," Ze added, "and we don't need anything foreign." And so every day, his troops did their demanding job. And even as they sustained losses, they gained back from Russia other Ukrainian towns it had taken. "We will do that every day," Ze had said, and it became impossible *not* to believe him.

It was a long, protracted battle, but day by day, Ukrainians walked the walk. Step by step, they defended what was theirs. It became inevitable that however long it took, "no matter how many servicemen get thrown there," the Ukrainian army would keep on keepin' on.

"Time is needed, patience is needed—our wisdom, energy, the ability to do your job to the maximum to come to victory," Ze had said in a video in the first month of war. "It is impossible to say how many more days it will take to liberate our Ukrainian land," he continued, "but it is possible to say that we will do that."

"We will definitely win, although no one expected that," he said a few months later.

And after a hundred days of battle, he reprised the first

war video he ever posted, of defiant government officials who were very much present in Kyiv, who had not fled as Putin had expected. "The armed forces of Ukraine are here," he repeated in his June 3, 2022, clip. "Most important, our people—the people of our nation—are here. We have been defending our country for a hundred days already. Victory will be ours! Glory to Ukraine!"

Opportunity in the Rubble

Zelenskyy's faith is what kept him doing his job "to the maximum to come to victory." His belief that "no matter how fierce the battles are, there's no chance for death to defeat life," as he had told Ukrainians on the Eastern Orthodox Good Friday. His belief in himself and in the strength and will of his people also reenergized those same people to keep on going. It was a spiral of faith, if you will, where a defiant leader who believed in his country helped that country keep believing in itself. And from a positive spiral like that, it was easier to see the light. A light that insisted on hope, even in the devastation.

Ze told his citizens that rebuilding their land from the depths of destruction was a challenge that carried with it a huge opportunity. "We are fighting to build a new Ukraine" is how he put it when he was speaking to Canadian university students. He explained that rebuilding from scratch—which, of course, would not have been the way he, or any Ukrainian, would have chosen it—gave them the chance to start fresh. They could restructure the country in a better, more practical and just way, from infrastructure to salaries for government workers to economic opportunity. They'd finally be able to break free from the stain of Soviet backwardness and corruption. And in a postwar rebirth, they could create the nation they've been vying for.

In fact, Ukraine became "a new nation that emerged on February 24 at 4 a.m.," Zelenskyy declared, "not born, but reborn."

This shift in perception that the president was espousing—the shift from overwhelm to opportunity—is such a boon to any person, organization, or country forced to scrap the old and bring in the better. Because while most of us will not need to rebuild our lives after a devastating war (let's hope), we'll all need to rebuild something at some point. And we must all take on tasks and projects of huge scope and workload from time to time.

I mean, think of the ordinary scope of starting a family, even—of creating a home, of having and raising children—or of starting over when couples and households and companies break up. And how many immigrants and refugees have had to begin a completely new life in a foreign country? I get the overwhelm.

So much of life can be overwhelming if we look at it as such. Or it can be seen as filled with both challenges and opportunities.

Choose your perspective, choose your life.

Perceptional Shakeups

Gleaning opportunity in the rubble is like shaking up the snow globe of our lives so that, suddenly, we see how we can make the most of our return to square one—a restart we hadn't necessarily asked for but had been given nonetheless. It's what is needed so that our suffering is not wasted but rather used as the seed of greatness.

"Ukraine has become the master of its own life and must decide for itself how to live," Ze said in a nightly video in May 2022. "Now is the time when we have the opportunity to build the future for Ukraine that we really want. . . . Without any obsolete and toxic things that have nothing to do with our national needs and our character."

Another perceptional shakeup that shifts our suffering is the ability to mine the rubble for the lessons—so that what's happened to us does not happen again.

"We must . . . learn to act preventively," as Ze pointed out in a virtual address to the 2022 Copenhagen Democracy Summit. "Not just to react, but to act as soon as words of aggression are heard. When it becomes clear that war can start at any moment. The aggressor must feel the power of the democratic world," he added, "the power of international law as soon as he intends to violate the existing basic norms.

"We should not be afraid, we should be prepared," is how he put it in a CNN interview, "and not just Ukraine but all the world."

He also spoke of letting go of the resentments and disagreements that had existed before the major calamity of war. "We must resolve disputes and remove the pressure of the past from our current relations with all Ukraine's neighbors—who respect us and are not occupiers of our state," he said. Zelenskyy was full of plans for his country's betterment, and these plans had no room or use for old grudges.

His peace-based vision of a bright postwar future in Ukraine not only helped his people withstand the war, but united the free world in upholding this vision and in promising to support it. By seeing the opportunity to build better, to be more prepared going forward, and to embrace a fresh start for international relations, Ze gave us the very blueprint we can use in our own lives to build, create, and re-create great things.

Word by Word

This is the second book I am writing. And like many people, I once considered writing a book an overwhelming undertaking. Just the sheer amount of thoughts and of words and pages that needed to be put together. Ugh. I can remember the feeling of panic that I used to experience at the very idea of it. And yet somewhere within me the desire to write books always lurked, waiting for its shot once I gathered enough pluck or moxie or whatever to actually try.

Now, my book is but a placeholder for your business idea or for that trip around the world or . . . fill in the blank. It is any large undertaking that seems undoable when you think of it as one giant blob of work. But as Ze has taught us, *Don't be afraid of the scope.* Approach the amorphous unknown one step; one word; one small, effective effort at a time.

If the Ukrainian soldiers could defend their land day after day, with no end in sight, then surely we can chip away at big projects and dreams little by little, for as long as it takes. For any undertaking, "time is needed, patience is needed," as Zelenskyy had said about eventual victory. But also, faith along with a shift in perspective are needed. This shift helps us see that every wee effort taken from a place of can-do will get us there. Even if "it is impossible to say how many more days it will take."

And this little-by-little attitude is what allows us to pick ourselves back up again, rather than languishing in that victim space we discussed. It allows us to rebuild ourselves and our lives as needed, and to keep returning to the task indefinitely. Rome wasn't built in a day, as they say. Neither will Ukraine be rebuilt in a day.

So whatever happens in your life, whatever gets broken, remember that one brick at a time is all you need to think about to put everything back together again. And you can learn from it all and do it better and become stronger and wiser and, dare I say, happier than before. That is the light within the darkness of loss and destruction.

Follow the light.

20

Alchemize

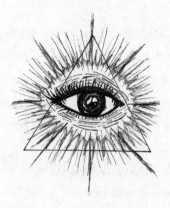

Ukraine *was* beautiful, but now it will become great. Great Ukraine.

> —*Zelenskyy said in a video posted after nearly a month of Russian destruction.*

I'm sure you've heard of alchemy before, but have you pondered it? This ability to turn sh*t into gold. Better yet, have you experienced it?

Because this type of sorcery is available to all of us, once we connect to our power source, our essence, our Inner Zelenskyy.

The concept of spiritual alchemy emerged in various

parts of the world in ancient times and has offered humans hope ever after. It gave us, mere earthlings, the understanding that anything, no matter how much darkness, depravity, and pain it endures, can be transformed into something else—something better. And this idea of transmutation has helped us find our way through both the personal and the collective experiences of the dark night of the soul, or utter desolation.

The basis of alchemy is that as we disintegrate into darkness, our brightest essence remains—everything else burns away. And from our bright essence yet more brightness eventually emerges, until we are far greater than we had ever been. What was metal—through fire and distress—is turned into gold.

In the words of Volodymyr Zelenskyy, "Ukraine *was* beautiful, but now it will become great."

Great Ukraine

This idea of turning pain, turning our darkest times, into greatness is extremely powerful. It is what allows us to heal with purpose.

"One can destroy the walls but cannot destroy the foundation on which the morale stands—the morale of our warriors, the morale of the entire country," Zelenskyy said at the Sofia Cathedral. "Don't let fury destroy us from within," he added, calling upon the forces inside and beyond him. "Turn it into a force for good to defy the forces of evil."

Turning "evil" into "good," or sh*t into gold, is the very

basis of alchemic transformation. It is the belief that all hardships, all tragedy, can be used as fuel for growth and to induce metamorphosis.

The enemy tried to crush Ukraine but Ukraine only grew stronger in its resolve for freedom, opportunity, and peace. More so, as the buildings and towns that were Ukraine crumbled to the ground, the heart of its people beamed bright in all its glory.

As I scoured Zelenskyy's Instagram feed during the war—as well as the feeds of other notable Ukrainians—I was floored by photographs of utter humanity: Ukrainian soldiers cradling stray cats, feeding famished dogs, and playing the piano in bombed-out schools . . . regular citizens helping each other get by, undeterred children continuing to play, even as they are surrounded by rubble.

It was as if the war, with all its atrocities, could only burn away the exterior, allowing us to clearly see the purity of the Ukrainian people—the naked virtue of true humanness from which it was impossible to look away. Houses, businesses, and unfortunately people were destroyed, but humanity itself shone ever brighter. For one can destroy the walls but not the foundation.

This beauty, this Ukrainian heart that remained and showed itself clearer than ever, had been distilled in its time of inordinate stress, if we're to look at the situation alchemically. And what Zelenskyy innately understood is that this was Ukraine's chance, this was its first step of building its greatest iteration yet.

The Ukrainian president urged his people to remember that we *always* have a choice, no matter what's being done unto us—we always have the choice to align with our own goodness and to transform destruction into brilliance. It was this very ability, this shift in perception, that helped him embrace the opportunity inherent in starting over. It's this acuity that helped him energize his citizens, as well as the rest of the world, in supporting the vision of a Great Ukraine.

Zelenskyy used Ukraine's exposed heart and purity of purpose as the basis from which to build its greatness.

So what would this Great Ukraine look like? What was needed to bring it to life—along with the end of war, of course?

Well, it would preferably be part of the European Union— that big dream whose seeds were finally being planted amid the war as the EU granted Ukraine candidate status. Because an alchemized Ukraine would certainly be an economic partner to its European neighbors; and it would continue to be an important food source for other countries and continents. It would be a technological innovator—in fact, its tech sector thrived even in war. Most important, it would be sovereign, liberated, and stable. And it would be rebuilt in a thought-out way. For "We are developing a comprehensive plan that provides for the reconstruction of what's destroyed, the modernization of state structures and the maximum acceleration of Ukraine's development," Ze said in April 2022.

Ukraine would be the gold that calcined after the fire.

An Alchemized Russia?

Now, the other part that alchemized during the war that Russia launched in Ukraine—a part which, perhaps could not be seen so clearly—is the morality and conscience within the bones of the rest of the world, or at least much of it, including in bits and pieces of the barricaded heart of Russia itself. Even as a deranged Putin and his cronies waged a cruel war and greatly suppressed their critics, those who breathed truth would not stay silent.

For example, "When the war started I promised that I won't flee," said the prominent Russian opposition politician Ilya Yashin, "and I will be saying the truth as long as I can. I don't want to make it easier for them. I don't want to hide from people that I despise and run away from war criminals." He became one of thousands of Russian citizens punished by the Kremlin for speaking out against the war.

There was the television employee who held up a sign that read "Stop the War" on live TV in Russia and was subsequently arrested and interrogated.

"I am thankful to those Russians who do not stop trying to convey the truth," President Zelenskyy stated in Russian following her actions, "to those who fight disinformation and tell the truth—real facts to their friends and loved ones. . . . And personally to the woman who entered the studio of Channel One with a poster against the war."

A few months later, the Moscow counselor Alexei Gorinov was sentenced to seven years in prison for continuing to openly speak out against Putin's aggression—despite his government's crackdown on critics—pointing out that "Children were dying." Even as he was being tried in court, he held up signs that read "I am against the war" and "Do you still need this war?" and, after his sentencing, he was applauded in the courtroom by regular Russian citizens—a small act of their own defiance. In his statement, Gorinov said, "War, whatever synonym you call it, is the last, dirtiest, vile thing, unworthy of the title of a man."

The already jailed opposition leader Alexei Navalny, whose own father hailed from the Chernobyl area, also spoke in court as he lost his appeal, with words aimed at Putin: "You will suffer a historic defeat in this stupid war that you started. It has no purpose or meaning. Why are we fighting a war?"

There were many other politicians, journalists, performers, not to mention everyday people, who spoke up and were made examples of for speaking up against the atrocities unleashed by Putin's regime—or who had to run from their homeland in order to escape prosecution. And it's easy for us to overlook them, because so many did *not* speak up, or even spoke in support of their government. But I don't want to focus on those who'd been brainwashed and led away from their own humanity. Let us instead look at the people who offer hope—for in hope lies the possibility of alchemy.

As Gorinov said at the end of his court statement, "I wish one day to become a future Russian ambassador to Ukraine."

*　　*　　*

The bravery of those who did not keep quiet but who put their very lives on the line to go against an oppressive government that was doing terrible things—well, that bravery is too the gold being molded in the fire of terror, as improbable as it sounds.

Since war is so tragic and dark, the very idea of alchemizing from its furnace may seem as far off as the idea of a someday Russian ambassador to Ukraine. But as our man Ze has taught us, "Everything is possible."

And while the Ukrainian heart shone bright, Russia's conscience too could be found amid its insanity, no matter how much Putin tried to punish, jail, and mute it. And Ze was thankful for that conscience and appealed to it many a time, saying things like, "Living in the Russian Federation is like virtual reality, like a video game. Come back to the world. It's more beautiful and more truthful."

Zelenskyy understood that the salvation of his country—and perhaps of the entire world—lay in both the dignified, ever-strengthened spirit that could never be destroyed in Ukraine, and in the stubborn conscience within the borders of its enemy.

The beginnings of alchemy exist in both the former and the latter—it's just that the stronger those dark forces, the greater the burn.

Personal Alchemy

The secret to alchemy, then, is to look toward the light, always—and to see the seeds of opportunity within the destruction, the seeds of wisdom within the pain, and the seeds of humanity within the seemingly inhumane.

Light and possibility are always present, even in the worst of circumstances. And when you focus on the light . . . well, what you focus on expands. The pain, tragedy, and hardship are then transformed. "Ukraine *was* beautiful, but now it will become great."

But the trick is to see the greatness even when most aren't there yet—when most are still blind to it. For that, we have forward thinkers like Zelenskyy. For that, we cultivate the forward thinker within. Because the question beckons, *Can you too alchemize your pain and hardships? Can you too find a path toward your own style of greatness?*

Finding opportunity in the lowest of times is a huge lesson for each of us—as we learned in the previous chapter. And in uncovering that opportunity, in using it, we forge a path toward better, stronger versions of ourselves.

Can we view what we overcome as a gift, then? Not just the overcoming part but even the suffering itself? For as we live, as we struggle, as we grow, we develop a blueprint for alchemizing this suffering. Low points and periods (decades, even) can mark an inception—like Zelenskyy and the Ukrainian people have demonstrated.

So let us seek out hope even as we wade through the darkness, and let us allow that darkness to shape us and transmute us.

After the furnace, only gold remains. Only will, only humanity, only light.

21

Choose Contentment

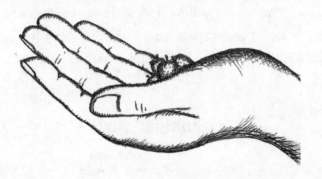

"We do not have a huge territory—from ocean to ocean, we do not have nuclear weapons, we do not fill the world market with oil and gas," *Zelenskyy posted on his social media channels a month into the war.* "But we have our people and our land. For us it is gold."

Zelenskyy passionately appreciated the people who made up his country more than any leader we as a world have witnessed in a long time. "We have our people and our land. For us it is gold," he wrote alongside pictures of Ukrainians—photos of them banding together to evacuate the weak, to deal with the damage of war . . . a shot of a soldier in uniform gently stroking an emaciated kitty.

The combination of gentleness and strength that we saw

in Zelenskyy was a mirror to that of Ukraine itself. A country that "won't give up anything Ukrainian," and doesn't "need anything foreign," as he had put it. A nation satisfied to simply be itself: "The free people of independent Ukraine."

As Ze explained in a 2022 interview with David Letterman, the very colors of the Ukrainian flag symbolize its values. The bottom yellow is for its land and its grain. "And this to me," the president said, "this blue color is a color of life, a color of the sky, space, and freedom."

Another Way

This notion of living freely and honorably that Ukraine was fighting to preserve was quite the contrast, not just to Russia with its imperialist aggression, but to many other nations and people (I won't name names) who've become so focused on bigger, better, faster. Because more money, more power, more speed is still very much the wheel that runs our modern machine—this idea that "better" is right around the corner, that whatever is missing can be plugged up with the next purchase or acquisition.

But in watching Ukraine, in watching Zelenskyy, we were being presented with another way.

"The Ukrainian people and their courage inspired the whole world," Ze said after half a year of fighting. "They gave humanity new hope that justice has not completely left our cynical world. And it is still not force that wins in it, but truth. Not money, but values. Not oil, but people."

Time and time again, Ze spoke of the gratification of his people and his state to be themselves. His country didn't want expansion or power or to "fill the world market with oil and gas." It just wanted freedom and harmony and the ability to live fruitfully. "We want simple and clear things," he said, "to liberate our land, to guarantee the safety of our people, to give peace to Ukrainians."

And yes, many of Ze's citizens also yearned to westernize and modernize and to dwell in opportunity—but those desires too were so sincere that we were reminded of the purity of our own origins.

Ukrainian goals and dreams were in such disparity to the power-hunger and the greed we saw in the Russian autocrats and oligarchs, but also, unfortunately, to our own collective consumerist hunger.

The photos of elderly Ukrainians taking care of their gardens, even as explosions took place not far off, really drove this point home. It was as if in those bright red berries within their cupped, weathered hands lay the answers for us all. For sometimes it's in the face of war and tragedy that we can actually grasp the importance of appreciating exactly what we have.

So can the rest of us—individuals and collectives—get better at embracing our lives and our freedoms? Right now, in this moment, can we want what we have . . . can we pause the constant chase for bigger and better? And can we do so without tragedy or oppression taking it all away first?

The Lack Principle

There is a story of a young Volodymyr Zelenskyy that captures what it was like to exist in the Soviet Union as the monolith was collapsing—what it was to want things just beyond your grasp, and how that wanting bore ingenuity.

The young Ze loved everything Western, cool, free, as did his friends and most of his Soviet-turned-ex-Soviet peers. And there was a period during which a lot of this Western stuff became more visible, more present, but still ridiculously beyond what most people could afford. I remember my childhood friend writing me from our suddenly free Riga about how much she wanted the exorbitant bananas she now saw in stores—fruit we used to see and obtain only once a year, if that, when our fathers sewed jeans and jean jackets on the side and sold them on the black market for some extra rubles.

Ze was thirteen when the USSR fell, and his "bananas" were jeans, actually (but the real, not the black-market, kind).

While Ze and a buddy of his were unable to afford their own pairs of the coveted American jeans all teens wanted there, they scraped together enough money to manage a pair between the two of them. The friends then painstakingly shared their jeans, alternating wearing them on dates and on other occasions. And you know what? They probably got more joy out of that sole pair than most of us get out of any item of clothing in our closets.

This lack that was inherent in the USSR and in the discombobulated years following its fall—well, it shaped you. A single dress, a single pair of shoes, and the inability to attain more, until the ability miraculously presented itself—and then the utter joy at that miraculous attainment.

My daughters love my stories of how I wore just plain white underwear to the beach in Latvia until I came to America, because there were no kids' bathing suits behind the Iron Curtain—they didn't exist. But then this one time in early perestroika, my babushka finally got permission to visit her sister in Israel and brought me back days-of-the-week undies with pretty pictures. As I proudly pulled up my skirt in school to show my friends my new undergarments, the *oohs* and *ahhs* that followed were almost like a shared joy.

Volodymyr Zelenskyy—the simple yet brilliant man who emerged from the land of no jeans or fancy undies—understood both the importance of access to nice things and the importance of valuing them, rather than rushing for something else.

I'm not suggesting we go chuck our denim or anything—unless it's because leggings and sweats are superior—or that we artificially impose lack upon ourselves. But it is a fact that contrast creates context, and that living through lack allows one to better appreciate abundance. This perspective—the perspective of struggle—makes it easier for us to be thankful for what we do have, instead of yearning and hustling indefinitely. . . . Well, sometimes it does. Other times, no matter how much we try to fill the hole we'd once lived in, we fall short.

And the thing is, whether we hail from Soviet lack or

American abundance, there is nothing outside of us that can fill that hole. So isn't it time to change our methods altogether?

Different Packaging

We're not all born into as little as was available in the Soviet Union, but we *do* all struggle at one point or another. And we all have stories of our human ancestors and what they had gone through, what they had endured before us (i.e., the Great Depression in America). We have plenty of examples of little to allow us to appreciate the lot we do have. We need only to remind ourselves.

And struggle, of course, comes in a variety of packaging also—one's lack of clothes is another's lack of love, for example. It's just that in the land(s) of plenty we've fallen under the mistaken impression that stuff can fill emotional scarcity. But news flash: it can't. And it can't fix a country's problems, either. In Ukraine, their people and their land are their gold. What is our gold in America? What is your gold within your company? Within your family? Within the privacy of your own heart?

Through a shift in perspective, greed and power can stop being the motivating forces of the world—as Zelenskyy has taught us, there is much reason to put values over profit. But this shift toward enoughness—away from the never-ending "more"—begins on a personal level.

You Are Enough

Being able to be content, valuing what you have, is such a vital staple of happiness. When more of us appreciate the simplicity of living in peace and in freedom—with the ability to change course, to pick ourselves back up after falling, to start anew—well . . . we can live with more ease and gratitude, to start. Which is perfect because the world, as it happens, transforms one person at a time.

So the work here—the work to get to that place of wanting what we do have, of appreciating it—it begins right where you are, exactly in the messiness and the imperfection of your life.

Right at this moment, can you list off the top of your head everything you're grateful for? Not what you're after, but what you *have*—including your own strengths and abilities?

As the Tao Te Ching teaches us, "Be content. Rest in your own fullness. When you realize there's nothing lacking, the whole world belongs to you."

And you know what? There's a paradoxical secret that is revealed to you when you cultivate contentment, whether you're an entity or a person. The secret is, when you embrace all you have and focus on the having—and on appreciating the having—well, that's when achieving further goals becomes easier. Because you're not looking for something to make you whole—*you already are, right?*—you're able to attract things and opportunities from a place of wholeness and of contentment. That's when your being expands, your possibilities grow, your Inner Ze gets his standing ovation. . . .

Volodymyr Zelenskyy is one of the best examples of an achiever the world has right now. And yet there's such a different quality to his achievement than, say, to that of Vladimir Putin, who coldly schemed his way to becoming a czar of sorts. The difference here is that Zelenskyy lined up with who he already was—his talent, his comedic ability, his charisma—and this allowed him to achieve the stardom he enjoyed for years. And then he once again lined up with the cause that called to him—the betterment of his country, which summoned him naturally through his comedy.

"I started out making fun of politicians, parodying them," he has said, pointing out that historically "jesters were allowed to tell the truth in ancient kingdoms." His jestering, though—the comedy he so loved—eventually cast him in the wartime leadership role that touched the heart of the entire world.

Ze's power, his achievement, stemmed from his very fullness. It came from his contentment with himself and the lot he'd been handed in life—his lot to uplift and then to lead Ukraine . . . his lot to, one day, lead us all.

22

Understand Victory

Victory is possible if you remember what honor is and do not deviate from your principles.

—*Zelenskyy recalling the example of Winston Churchill, when receiving Britain's Churchill Society's Leadership Award*

Victory is the goal of every battle that ever was or ever will be—every war, every disease, every struggle. But what this end goal actually entails is the understanding that it is not an end at all, but a foundation. Which is why we must keep in mind not only what we want to overcome, but what we want to create thereafter—that is the *why* of our intended victory, the *why* of why we are fighting and sacrificing and even dying for it.

But one point Zelenskyy never seemed to waver on, as a wartime leader, is that victory would, in fact, belong to Ukraine. It was not a matter of *if* but a matter of *eventually*. "All Ukrainians must remember one thing," he said many months after Russia's invasion: "No matter what, we are heading toward victory—in spite of everything." And this belief in eventual triumph was shared by the bulk of his countrymen and women, for there was no other way to exit a battle for one's own survival.

It's as if Ze, together with the Ukrainian army and every-day folks who refused to give up . . . it's as if they all spoke this triumph into being. "We will make our way to victory, it will happen," Zelenskyy pronounced on Ukraine's Inde-pendence Day, eyes ablaze.

Such steadfastness attracted support from around the world, and the support made Ukraine's win ever more possible (and just remember that at the start it seemed utterly *im*possible—all the war analysts said as much). Ukrainians—with Zelenskyy at the helm—drew victory onto themselves; they manifested it with their will, their spirit, and their very being. Though Ze also never lost sight of the bigger-than-war picture.

Big Picture

As I write this, I do not know what Ukraine's ultimate victory will look like—remember the caveat at the start of this book.

But I've learned to heed the way of Zelenskyy, who tells us that "patience on the way to victory" is necessary. Because patience is not about waiting; patience is about knowing. It is grounded in the kind of unwavering faith that permeated every word Ze spoke to the world throughout the conflict.

"No one knows today how much time and effort it will take to reach it," he declared virtually to the audience at the International Churchill Society in Britain. "However, the victory is worth the effort."

And to him, it was not just about winning a war and declaring a free, sovereign Ukraine once again—though, of course, this was the pressing objective. Still, "War cannot be won by victories," he had told the United Nations back in 2019, quoting the writing of Ernest Hemingway, "for the one who wins the war never stops fighting."

Zelenskyy had long spoken of the awfulness of fighting, before it took over his existence so fully—and he spoke of the need to prevent it. "For any war today—in Ukraine, Syria, Libya, Yemen, or any other corner of the planet, regardless of the number of casualties—is the greatest threat to the entire civilization," he'd told the United Nations. Winning for him, then, was making war less of a possibility—even as he and his were living through its horror.

"We are fighting together to ensure that war is never again seen by any aggressor as a means of achieving aggressive goals," he told Britain. "And perhaps for the first time in the history of mankind, we are now able to show everyone in the world—and for ages—that democracies, united, can stop any tyranny, even if at first it seems that it has unlimited resources for aggression."

Zelenskyy took the long view when it came to victory—a view that didn't present a time frame (because that was not possible for a long while) but one that included the bigger picture of what the world could achieve in supporting Ukraine. He was able to clearly show America, Europe, and other countries why it was important for them to cast their chips with his nation—why Ukraine's triumph was so vital and, really, the only option.

By clarifying what he meant by winning, Ze made everyone want to win alongside him. He helped us understand that victory for Ukraine was the defeat of tyranny as a whole—it was a win for peace and for humankind.

Even in fighting a bloody war, Zelenskyy remained a pacifist.

Beyond War

Ze viewed victory for his country as a far wider endeavor than what took place on the front lines, and vaster, even, than defeating warmongers. He made it clear that what Ukraine represented in the global arena mattered too, and a lot. For he wanted the entire world to know how much Ukrainians had to offer—how much greater they were than the conflict that had been cast upon them.

"Today, victory in all directions is important for us," he told Australian university students in August 2022, "not only on the battlefield."

He told them how vital culture, sports, and sciences were in times of fighting. "Maybe even more important than in times of peace." As he explained, "For Ukraine, for every citizen today, victory is motivation." And he was referring to triumphs that span all modalities.

"We cheer for our athletes like never before. We cheer for our cultural figures, and Eurovision is not an exception, but, on the contrary, a great example," he said, referring to Kalush Orchestra's win in the popular European competition.

And Ze strongly supported not just the work of well-known Ukrainians, but also of those in less famous careers. *All* work was vital for Ukraine's future. "We cheer for our scientists," he said, "and when they become the best mathematicians or physicists in the world, we cheer for them more than ever. Some of us did not even know about such people in peacetime."

He explained that in wartime, every arena was a battlefield against needless aggression. Every sphere of influence counted, and celebrating Ukraine's contributions was more significant than ever—not despite the war, but in order to transcend it.

Paradoxical Purpose

There are times in life when we are cast in undesirable situations where we simply must do what needs doing—like winning a war you did not start, in Zelenskyy's case, along with all of the ancillary activities necessary to bring forth this eventual victory. As he had put it when he got elected (with a more contained conflict being the Ukrainian reality for years by then), "History is unfair, it's true. It wasn't us who started this war, but it is us who will have to stop it."

Because accepting what is—the situation right in front of you—is necessary in order to move forward. Accepting even the unacceptable is step one. And many steps fall between that first one and ultimate success. Just as long as you "do not deviate from your principles," as Ze had said, you will be okay.

How do you, then, hold on to these principles when you are dragged into a situation you do not desire? How do you deal with what is and remain yourself?

Here, once again, we turn to our Inner Zelenskyy.

For victory, as Ze has shown us, is about seeing the bigger picture amid a crappy situation. It's about glimpsing the eventual good that you can achieve by dealing with these undesirable circumstances. It's about embracing the paradoxical fact that by going through darkness you can usher in even more light. And it is about recognizing your job as a carrier of this light.

Carry the Light

"Even in the darkest of circumstances, there are people who carry light," Zelenskyy had said on the Day of Remembrance of Ukrainians who saved Jews in World War II. And present-day Ukrainians have gotten plenty of experience with both figurative and literal darkness in this war—there were periods when Russia pulverized Ukraine's infrastructure, leaving millions of people without power.

But, "even in total darkness, we will find each other" their president proclaimed in a Christmas address. "And if there is no heat, we will give a big hug to warm each other."

Makes you wonder—in any dark circumstance, whether national, global, or personal—can we too choose to find each other and to carry the light?

Carriers of the light know of their inevitable triumph over darkness, and they walk their course regardless of how long it takes. They are patient—or rather they choose patience over and over again—and they are steady (well, mostly). They recognize what they're working toward, their faith is solid, and they keep on keepin' on.

So as we support Ukrainians in winning a war they did not want—and doing so in a way that helps wars become less of a possibility in the world—let us remember to also glance at ourselves.

What victory are *you* walking toward? Where would you benefit from holding on to your integrity and just keepin' on?

Dust off your faith if you've lost it—it's a far more useful robe than hopelessness. Walk toward your own triumph, however long it takes. And know that no matter what, it is possible—*everything* is possible.

Whatever you are or will be dealing with, remember to treat your victorious objective as just the beginning. Cultivate a vision for yourself that is grander than your trials, tribulations, and mishaps. See beyond your lowest moments and let part of you dwell in that vastness at all times, even during the undesirable ones—or especially then.

As you move forward, stick to your principles. Stick to your honor, to your vision, to your Inner Zelenskyy. Then you too will be a beacon of hope—first of all, for yourself, and then for everyone and everything you encounter.

Epilogue

It can be difficult to end a book whose hero is still hard at work, still leading the way. But rather than looking at it as an ending, I see it as a pause. A moment to take in the lessons he's been bestowing upon the world. A moment to digest these lessons and apply them to our institutions and our lives.

Because I suspect we'll have an eye on Zelenskyy for years to come (fingers crossed). He is a once-in-a-generation sort of person who has been gifted to us—the humans of the earth—despite himself. As he said in his April 2022 *Time* interview, "I've gotten older. . . . I've aged from all this wisdom that I never wanted.

"It's the wisdom tied to the number of people who have died, and the torture the Russian soldiers perpetrated. That kind of wisdom . . ." he added, trailing off. "To be honest, I never had the goal of attaining knowledge like that."

Sometimes, though, such is life, isn't it? Where you're thrust into situations that you couldn't have predicted, and definitely wouldn't have chosen, but there you are. You are there. And then what you do with it all is what matters. What you do then, how you choose to be, makes all the difference.

Leading Ukraine through war and through atrocities wasn't Zelenskyy's goal. But it *was* his fate. And the rest of the world—we are the beneficiaries of what he did thereafter. We are the beneficiaries of what he did and who he be'ed with the war he'd been handed.

Here's the thing: The bulk of us have not had a leader of Zelenskyy's caliber in a very long time, if ever in our lifetimes. And in this complicated existence of ours we instinctively yearn for such a leader. Yet it's as if the cynicism with which Ze often described Russia also became more of a reality for our collective state—and better summed up what we came to expect of politicians everywhere—quite contrary to the selflessness, the honor, the realness that the Ukrainian president epitomized.

But then, suddenly, there he was—thrust into a situation he definitely wouldn't have chosen—with the whole world watching. And finally, we all saw the leader we'd been yearning for.

So, yes, we are fortunate to have witnessed Volodymyr Zelenskyy's leadership—which shaped the course of history for Europe, and, really, for the whole world. We are fortunate to live in a time when we seamlessly got to hear his poignant words regularly and to drink in his faith and his courage. The world is certainly better for his very existence.

Still, let us not forget perhaps the greatest of Zelenskyy's teachings—the one that takes us from fan to equal: "Every one of us—*everyone*—is the leader of our time." For "I am not a politician, I am just a simple person who has come to break down this system."

Zelenskyy has shown that all of us, simple persons as we are, have the ability to break down outdated systems—even if only just a bit, even if simply in our own spheres of influence . . . even though we must begin within the privacy of our homes, our minds, our hearts.

And sometimes there will be failures and mistakes in our endeavors and in our personal lives; no matter. What the unlikely Ukrainian hero has shown us, in all his extraordinary ordinariness—what can help get us off our sulking couch when needed—is that we each have an ounce of Zelenskyy within us. We each have more potentialities than we realize in our moments (or years) of ennui. We can each tap into our limitlessness.

What's being asked of us is not perfection but intention, not superiority but humanity.

Let us make our way forward then, each one of us rising up as best we can to be the very leaders and caretakers that our souls are calling for. Let us light the way no matter the scope—for our children need beacons, as do our friends and our communities. And then, as Ze said when he was granted the Churchill Society's Leadership Award, "It will become our shared history, so outstanding that you and I will later be quoted in the same way that we are now quoting Sir Churchill."

And so it shall be.

*   *   *

"Putin's war of conquest is failing," US President Biden declares in Kyiv. He is visiting the Ukrainian capital a year into the war, as the city defiantly brims with life. "Kyiv stands," he says. "And Ukraine stands. Democracy stands."

And as I write this in May of 2023, Kyiv stands stronger than ever, thwarting an unprecedented volley of aerial attacks from Russia night after night. Simultaneously, President Zelenskyy is touring the world, briskly and intently—Europe, Saudi Arabia, the G7 summit in Japan—to shore up support for Ukraine's imminent counteroffensive . . . All the support in the world is needed for this anticipated push by Ukrainians to kick Russian forces out of their country.

I'd love to write here that the counteroffensive does the job once and for all—that the entirety of Ukraine is liberated, independent, and victorious over Putin's forces of autocracy. But we are not up to that yet. And, like all wars before it, this one is not predictable. Plus, it has already lasted too long.

So, how much more time is needed to free every bit of Ukrainian land occupied by the Russian Federation?

How much more tragedy will Ukrainians incur as the aggressors cruelly snuff out civilian lives in bombing after bombing? How many more lost soldiers, how many more ruins, how many more dashed dreams?

How much more bloodshed and destruction until peace is restored?

The questions and variables are endless. But the answer stands the same:

"We do not yet know the date of our victory," says Volodymyr Zelenskyy on May 8, Victory in Europe Day (which marks the end of WWII), "but we know that it will be a holiday for all of Ukraine, for all of Europe, for the entire free world . . . It should be like this and will be."

Man, do I believe him wholeheartedly! I am awed by his faith and I imbue my own life with it; I let it seep into even the Soviet-era fiber of my being.

I urge you to try it out for yourself. I urge you to also try on Zelenskyy's defiant faith for size—his faith and his can-do attitude; his courage and his humility; his chutzpah and his graciousness. Try it despite all the negativity that abounds . . . or because of it.

"Darkness could not overcome our spirit," Zelenskyy tells us on Easter, 2023.

"On the morning of February 24, a dark night began," he says, "And at the same time, our awakening began."

Can you feel it? This awakening.

Let yourself feel it. You don't need to wait for anything else, not even for the end of war.

Right now, close your eyes. Take a breath. Connect to your Inner Zelenskyy, and let yourself awaken.

Acknowledgments

The main person to acknowledge here is obviously the Ukrainian president. I never planned to write a book like this; it's just that his caliber of character had to be written about—so I did my little part. And my editor, Elizabeth Beier, understood this and quickly enriched my vision. I am so grateful to her and to everyone at St. Martin's who has supported the book, as well as to my agent, Lisa Hagan.

Thanks also to my husband and girls, because without them, who even am I? And to my friends and family and readers who expressed enthusiasm for my work—I needed it.

Finally, thank you, Mom and Dad, for getting me the hell out of the Soviet Union!

Slava Ukraini!

Rodrigo Cid

JESSIE ASYA KANZER is the award-winning author of *Don't Just Sit There, DO NOTHING*. She was born in the Soviet Union and left at age eight. A former reporter and actress, she once found herself on set of a Zelensky film and has been following his story ever since. Kanzer's writing has appeared in *The New York Times, USA Today, The Washington Post,* and many other publications. She lives with her husband, two daughters, and two cats in Dobbs Ferry, NY.